Helpful Guide To Understanding "The Chosen" Season Four

Dr. Rick Gillespie-Mobley

DEDICATION

I dedicate this book first to my son Marjoe Milliner who was unknown to me as my son for the first 49 years of his life. I treasure the day we met on March 2nd, 2024 at 12 noon in Jamestown, NY at Bob Evans Restaurant. It was the conversation of a lifetime as we shared our lives together. What an amazing young man.

I also dedicate this book to my daughter, my son's wife Rebecca Wissmann Milliner, whose pursuit of discovering the truth made it possible for my son, and I to be brought together. My wife and I look to having a blessed time with her in our lives. She is an incredible young woman.

I further dedicate this book to our granddaughter Chantre Mauro and her husband Matt and to our grandson Dantae Milliner. We look forward to being a part of their lives. We are in great anticipation of meeting our first great-grandchild, Theo.

I also dedicate this book to Rev. Dr. Toby Gillespie-Mobley who has been a faithful companion since August 30, 1980. My life could have never been what it has been without her. She is one of the most amazing examples of a person loving others for the cause of Jesus Christ that I have ever known. I thank God for everyday of our marriage these past 44 years.

I also dedicate it to our five children of whom we arc super proud. Our daughter Samantha Mobley who is a District Court Judge in Charlotte, NC. Our daughter Anita Allen (Milan) who is a teacher and educator in Montgomery, Al.

Our daughter Sharon Davison who is a health care professional in Cleveland, OH. Our son Keon Abner (Ashley) who is the pastor of Bridge City Church in Cleveland, OH. Our son Marjoe Millener (Rebecca) who is Supervisory Inventory Management Specialist in New York. The five of you have made us proud.

We thank God for all of our wonderful grandchildren and now even great grandchild. Your G-Ma and G-Pa love you all.

Lastly, I am grateful to our four-legged friends, three of the best dogs ever, who brought a lot of joy into our lives. They are Faith, Hope, and Berea. Berea has especially helped me to understand companionship in a way that has blessed my life. She truly is my shadow.

Special thanks to all of our church sons and daughters as well as all of our previous foster children. You were a blessing in our lives in more ways than you could ever imagine. You are now out there in the world making a difference. Never forget what we tried to teach you about the love God has for you in Jesus Christ. Remember, the fear of the Lord is the beginning of wisdom.

I hope this guide will help more people to benefit and enjoy one of the greatest Christian series the world has ever known. The Chosen allows you to see the heart and compassion of Jesus for all people in the world.

TABLE OF CONTENTS

Purpose Of This Book

One of the purposes of "The Chosen" is to create characters with a depth of life, so that you can read the scriptures and understand why biblical characters may behave in the way that they do. "The Chosen" is not a biblical story as revealed in the Scriptures, but it is a story that contains the Scriptures and provides us with a possibility of how things may have taken place. If you accept it for what it is, you will be strengthened and encouraged in your faith. If you demand it to be a literal rendition of the Scriptures, you will be disappointed in your search. "The Chosen" is a wonderful way to capture the heart, the emotions, and the essence of the characters in the Scriptures. It is outstanding in its presentation of characters of various racial and cultural backgrounds. It does more to promote racial harmony and equality within the body of Christ than any work I have seen before on the life of Christ.

The purpose of this book is to help you understand how the Scriptures are woven into the story and to learn from both the lives of the characters and the teachings of Scripture. By providing you with a summary of the main characters in each episode, a summary of the content of the episode, and the Scriptures referred to in the episode, you will be able to glean a greater understanding of what is happening as you watch. You will also be informed on which things in an episode are in the Scriptures and which are there simply for character development and storyline.

There are questions for discussion that you can use in a small group if you choose to use "The Chosen" as a Bible study topic. The questions do not require a scholarly background to lead the discussion. They are a combination of your reactions to the characters and your application of the Scriptures. The number of questions you will use will depend on the size of your group and whether or not you have watched the episodes prior to the meeting. Obviously, you will have more time for discussion if you watch the episodes prior to coming together.

The final purpose of this book is to help people come to know Jesus Christ as Lord and Savior of their lives through this remarkable film series. The episodes can be watched for free on the Chosen website at https://watch.thechosen.tv/. The episodes are also available for free on the Angel Studios App for phones and on the Angel Studio website at https://www.angel.com/watch/the-chosen. "The Chosen" episodes are available for purchase on Amazon.com on DVD.

Actual Biblical Characters Appearing In The Chosen

Seasons 1, 2, 3, and 4.

Abigail

Then David sent word to Abigail, asking her to become his wife. [40] His servants went to Carmel and said to Abigail, "David has sent us to you to take you to become his wife."[41] She bowed down with her face to the ground and said, "I am your servant and am ready to serve you and wash the feet of my lord's servants." [42] Abigail quickly got on a donkey and, attended by her five female servants, went with David's messengers and became his wife. *The New International Version* (Grand Rapids, MI: Zondervan, 2011), I Samuel 25:39-42

Ahimelek

14 Ahimelek answered the king, "Who of all your servants is as loyal as David, the king's son-in-law, captain of your bodyguard and highly respected in your household? 15 Was that day the first time I inquired of God for him? Of course not! Let not the king accuse your servant or any of his father's family, for your servant knows nothing at all about this whole affair." *The New International Version* (Grand Rapids, MI: Zondervan, 2011), 1 Sa 22:14–15.

Andrew

40 Andrew, Simon Peter's brother, was one of the two who heard what John had said and who had followed Jesus. 41 The first thing Andrew did was to find his brother Simon and tell him, "We have found the Messiah" (that is, the Christ). 42 And he brought him to Jesus. *The New International Version* (Grand Rapids, MI: Zondervan, 2011), Jn 1:40–42.

Bathsheba

24 Then David comforted his wife Bathsheba, and he went to her and made love to her. She gave birth to a son, and they named him Solomon. *The New International Version* (Grand Rapids, MI: Zondervan, 2011), 2 Sa 12:24.

Caiaphas

[49] Then one of them, named Caiaphas, who was high priest that year, spoke up, "You know nothing at all! [50] You do not realize that it is better for you that one man die for the people than that the whole nation perish."[51] He did not say this on his own, but as high priest that year he prophesied that Jesus would die for the Jewish nation, *The New International Version* (Grand Rapids, MI: Zondervan, 2011), John 11:49-50

Chuza

Joanna the wife of **Chuza**, the manager of Herod's household; Susanna; and many others. *The New International Version* (Grand Rapids, MI: Zondervan, 2011), Luke 8:3

Daniel

These were the sons of David born to him in Hebron: The firstborn was Amnon the son of Ahinoam of Jezreel; the second, Daniel the son of Abigail of Carmel; *The New International Version* (Grand Rapids, MI: Zondervan, 2011), 1 Chronicles 3:1

David

David went to Nob, to Ahimelek the priest. Ahimelek trembled when he met him, and asked, "Why are you alone? Why is no one with you?" 2 David answered Ahimelek the priest, "The king sent me on a mission and said to me, 'No one is to know anything about the mission I am sending you on.' As for my men, I have told them to meet me at a certain place. 3 Now then, what do you have on hand? Give me five loaves of bread, or whatever you can find." *The New International Version* (Grand Rapids, MI: Zondervan, 2011), 1 Sa 21:1–3.

Elizabeth

After this his wife Elizabeth became pregnant and for five months remained in seclusion. 25 "The Lord has done this for me," she said. "In these days he has shown his favor and taken away my disgrace among the people." *The New International Version* (Grand Rapids, MI: Zondervan, 2011), Luke 1:24-25

Herod

[17] For Herod himself had given orders to have John arrested, and he had him bound and put in prison. He did this because of Herodias, his brother Philip's wife, whom he had married. [18] For John had been saying to Herod, "It is not lawful for you to have your brother's wife." *The New International Version* (Grand Rapids, MI: Zondervan, 2011), Mark 6:17-18

Herodias

[19] So Herodias nursed a grudge against John and wanted to kill him. But she was not able to, [20] because Herod feared John and protected him, knowing him to be a righteous and holy man. *The New International Version* (Grand Rapids, MI: Zondervan, 2011), Mark 6:19-20

Jacob

5 So he came to a town in Samaria called Sychar, near the plot of ground Jacob had given to his son Joseph. 6 Jacob's well was there, and Jesus, tired as he was from the journey, sat down by the

well. It was about noon. *The New International Version* (Grand Rapids, MI: Zondervan, 2011), Jn 4:5–6.

Jairus

22 Then one of the synagogue leaders, named Jairus, came, and when he saw Jesus, he fell at his feet. 23 He pleaded earnestly with him, "My little daughter is dying. Please come and put your hands on her so that she will be healed and live." 24 So Jesus went with him. *The New International Version* (Grand Rapids, MI: Zondervan, 2011), Mk 5:22–24.

Jairus Daughter (Neelie)

After he put them all out, he took the child's father and mother and the disciples who were with him, and went in where the child was. 41 He took her by the hand and said to her, "Talitha koum!" (which means "Little girl, I say to you, get up!"). 42 Immediately the girl stood up and began to walk around (she was twelve years old). At this they were completely astonished. 43 He gave strict orders not to let anyone know about this, and told them to give her something to eat. *The New International Version* (Grand Rapids, MI: Zondervan, 2011), Mk 5:40–43.

James son of Alphaeus (Little James)
2 These are the names of the twelve apostles: first, Simon (who is called Peter) and his brother Andrew; James son of Zebedee, and his brother John; 3 Philip and Bartholomew; Thomas and Matthew the tax collector; James son of Alphaeus, and Thaddaeus; 4 Simon the Zealot and Judas Iscariot, who betrayed him.

James son of Zebedee (Big James)
21 Going on from there, he saw two other brothers, James son of Zebedee and his brother John. They were in a boat with their father Zebedee, preparing their nets. Jesus called them, 22 and immediately they left the boat and their father and followed

him.*The New International Version* (Grand Rapids, MI: Zondervan, 2011), Mt 4:21–22.

Jesus As Twelve Year Old

41 Every year Jesus' parents went to Jerusalem for the Festival of the Passover. 42 When he was twelve years old, they went up to the festival, according to the custom. 43 After the festival was over, while his parents were returning home, the boy Jesus stayed behind in Jerusalem, but they were unaware of it

Jesus

35 The next day John was there again with two of his disciples. 36 When he saw Jesus passing by, he said, "Look, the Lamb of God!" 37 When the two disciples heard him say this, they followed Jesus.*The New International Version* (Grand Rapids, MI: Zondervan, 2011), Jn 1:35–37.

Joanna

3 Joanna the wife of Chuza, the manager of Herod's household; Susanna; and many others. These women were helping to support them out of their own means. *The New International Version* (Grand Rapids, MI: Zondervan, 2011), Lk 8:2–3.

John

21 Going on from there, he saw two other brothers, James son of Zebedee and his brother John. They were in a boat with their father Zebedee, preparing their nets. Jesus called them, 22 and immediately they left the boat and their father and followed him. *The New International Version* (Grand Rapids, MI: Zondervan, 2011), Mt 4:21–22.

John The Baptist

In those days John the Baptist came, preaching in the wilderness of Judea 2 and saying, "Repent, for the kingdom of heaven has come near." 3 This is he who was spoken of through the prophet Isaiah:

"A voice of one calling in the wilderness, 'Prepare the way for the Lord, make straight paths for him.' " *The New International Version* (Grand Rapids, MI: Zondervan, 2011), Mt 3:1–3.

John The Baptist's Disciples
2 When John, who was in prison, heard about the deeds of the Messiah, he sent his disciples 3 to ask him, "Are you the one who is to come, or should we expect someone else?" *The New International Version* (Grand Rapids, MI: Zondervan, 2011), Mt 11:2–3.

Joseph
48 When his parents saw him, they were astonished. His mother said to him, "Son, why have you treated us like this? Your father and I have been anxiously searching for you." *The New International Version* (Grand Rapids, MI: Zondervan, 2011), Lk 2:48.

Judas Iscariot

4 But one of his disciples, Judas Iscariot, who was later to betray him, objected, 5 "Why wasn't this perfume sold and the money given to the poor? It was worth a year's wages." 6 He did not say this because he cared about the poor but because he was a thief; as keeper of the money bag, he used to help himself to what was put into it. *The New International Version* (Grand Rapids, MI: Zondervan, 2011), Jn 12:4–6.

Joshua

13 Then Moses set out with Joshua his aide, and Moses went up on the mountain of God *The New International Version* (Grand Rapids, MI: Zondervan, 2011), Ex 24:13.

Lazarus

9 Meanwhile a large crowd of Jews found out that Jesus was there and came, not only because of him but also to see Lazarus, whom he had raised from the dead. 10 So the chief priests made plans to kill Lazarus as well, 11 for on account of him many of the Jews were going over to Jesus and believing in him. _The New International Version_ (Grand Rapids, MI: Zondervan, 2011) John 12:9-11

Luke

Many have undertaken to draw up an account of the things that have been fulfilled among us, 2 just as they were handed down to us by those who from the first were eyewitnesses and servants of the word. 3 With this in mind, since I myself have carefully investigated everything from the beginning, I too decided to write an orderly account for you, most excellent Theophilus, 4 so that you may know the certainty of the things you have been taught. _The New International Version_ (Grand Rapids, MI: Zondervan, 2011), Lk 1:1–4.

Man Healed At The Pool Of Bethesda (Jesse)

5 Some time later, Jesus went up to Jerusalem for one of the Jewish festivals. 2 Now there is in Jerusalem near the Sheep Gate a pool, which in Aramaic is called Bethesda and which is surrounded by five covered colonnades. 3 Here a great number of disabled people used to lie—the blind, the lame, the paralyzed. [4] 5 One who was there had been an invalid for thirty-eight years. 6 When Jesus saw him lying there and learned that he had been in this condition for a long time, he asked him, "Do you want to get well?" _The New International Version_ (Grand Rapids, MI: Zondervan, 2011), Jn 5:1–6.

Man Healed In The Decapolis from deafness and being mute.

31 Then Jesus left the vicinity of Tyre and went through Sidon,

down to the Sea of Galilee and into the region of the Decapolis. 32 There some people brought to him a man who was deaf and could hardly talk, and they begged Jesus to place his hand on him. 33 After he took him aside, away from the crowd, Jesus put his fingers into the man's ears. Then he spit and touched the man's tongue. 34 He looked up to heaven and with a deep sigh said to him, "Ephphatha!" (which means "Be opened!"). 35 At this, the man's ears were opened, his tongue was loosened and he began to speak plainly. *The New International Version* (Grand Rapids, MI: Zondervan, 2011), Mk 7:31–35.

Man Healed Who Had Been Born Blind (Uzziah)

[13] They brought to the Pharisees the man who had been blind. [14] Now the day on which Jesus had made the mud and opened the man's eyes was a Sabbath. [15] Therefore the Pharisees also asked him how he had received his sight. "He put mud on my eyes," the man replied, "and I washed, and now I see." . *The New International Version* (Grand Rapids, MI: Zondervan, 2011), John 9:13-15

Martha

As Jesus and his disciples were on their way, he came to a village where a woman named **Martha** opened her home to him. She had a sister called Mary, who sat at the Lord's feet listening to what he said. But **Martha** was distracted by all the preparations that had to be made. She came to him and asked, "Lord, don't you care that my sister has left me to do the work by myself? Tell her to help me!" *The New International Version* (Grand Rapids, MI: Zondervan, 2011), Luke10:38-40

Mary (Jesus' Mother)

48 When his parents saw him, they were astonished. His mother said to him, "Son, why have you treated us like this? Your father

and I have been anxiously searching for you." *The New International Version* (Grand Rapids, MI: Zondervan, 2011), Lk 2:48.

Mary (Martha's & Lazarus's Sister)

3 Then Mary took about a pint[a] of pure nard, an expensive perfume; she poured it on Jesus' feet and wiped his feet with her hair. And the house was filled with the fragrance of the perfume. *The New International Version* (Grand Rapids, MI: Zondervan, 2011), John 12:3

Mary Magdalene

After this, Jesus traveled about from one town and village to another, proclaiming the good news of the kingdom of God. The Twelve were with him, 2 and also some women who had been cured of evil spirits and diseases: Mary (called Magdalene) from whom seven demons had come out; 3 Joanna the wife of Chuza, the manager of Herod's household; Susanna; and many others. These women were helping to support them out of their own means. *The New International Version* (Grand Rapids, MI: Zondervan, 2011), Lk 8:1–3.

Matthew

10 While Jesus was having dinner at Matthew's house, many tax collectors and sinners came and ate with him and his disciples. 11 When the Pharisees saw this, they asked his disciples, "Why does your teacher eat with tax collectors and sinners?" *The New International Version* (Grand Rapids, MI: Zondervan, 2011), Mt 9:10–11.

Moses

" So Moses prayed for the people. 8 The Lord said to Moses, "Make a snake and put it up on a pole; anyone who is bitten can look at it and live." 9 So Moses made a bronze snake and put it up on a pole. Then when anyone was bitten by a snake and looked at the bronze snake, they lived.

Nathanael

47 When Jesus saw Nathanael approaching, he said of him, "Here truly is an Israelite in whom there is no deceit." 48 "How do you know me?" Nathanael asked. Jesus answered, "I saw you while you were still under the fig tree before Philip called you." 49 Then Nathanael declared, "Rabbi, you are the Son of God; you are the king of Israel." 50 Jesus said, "You *The New International Version* (Grand Rapids, MI: Zondervan, 2011), Jn 1:47–50.

Nicodemus

"Now there was a Pharisee, a man named Nicodemus who was a member of the Jewish ruling council. 2 He came to Jesus at night and said, "Rabbi, we know that you are a teacher who has come from God. For no one could perform the signs you are doing if God were not with him."" *The New International Version* (Grand Rapids, MI: Zondervan, 2011), Jn 3:1–2.

38 Later, Joseph of Arimathea asked Pilate for the body of Jesus. Now Joseph was a disciple of Jesus, but secretly because he feared the Jewish leaders. With Pilate's permission, he came and took the body away. 39 He was accompanied by Nicodemus, the man who earlier had visited Jesus at night. Nicodemus brought a mixture of myrrh and aloes, about seventy-five pounds. 40 Taking Jesus' body, the two of them wrapped it, with the spices, in strips of linen. This was in accordance with Jewish burial customs *The New International Version* (Grand Rapids, MI: Zondervan, 2011), Jn 19:38–40.

Phillip

43 The next day Jesus decided to leave for Galilee. Finding Philip, he said to him, "Follow me." 44 Philip, like Andrew and Peter, was from the town of Bethsaida. 45 Philip found Nathanael and told him, "We have found the one Moses wrote about in the Law, and about whom the prophets also wrote—Jesus of Nazareth, the son of Joseph."*The New International Version* (Grand Rapids, MI: Zondervan, 2011), Jn 1:43–45.

Pilate

In the fifteenth year of the reign of Tiberius Caesar—when Pontius Pilate was governor of Judea, Herod tetrarch of Galilee, his brother Philip tetrarch of Iturea and Traconitis, and Lysanias tetrarch of Abilene—2 during the high-priesthood of Annas and Caiaphas, the word of God came to John son of Zechariah in the wilderness. *The New International Version* (Grand Rapids, MI: Zondervan, 2011), Lk 3:1–2.

Pilate's Wife

19 While Pilate was sitting on the judge's seat, his wife sent him this message: "Don't have anything to do with that innocent man, for I have suffered a great deal today in a dream because of him." *The New International Version* (Grand Rapids, MI: Zondervan, 2011), Mt 27:19.

Roman Centurion Whose Servant Was Healed (Gaius)

[5] When Jesus had entered Capernaum, a centurion came to him, asking for help. [6] "Lord," he said, "my servant lies at home paralyzed, suffering terribly." [7] Jesus said to him, "Shall I come and heal him?" [8] The centurion replied, "Lord, I do not deserve to have you come under my roof. But just say the word, and my servant will be healed. [9] For I myself am a man under authority, with soldiers under me. I tell this one, 'Go,' and he goes; and that one, 'Come,' and he comes. I say to my servant, 'Do this,' and he does

it." *The New International Version* (Grand Rapids, MI: Zondervan, 2011), Matthew 8:5-9

Salome (step daughter of King Herod)

When the daughter of Herodias came in and danced, she pleased Herod and his dinner guests. The king said to the girl, "Ask me for anything you want, and I'll give it to you." *The New International Version* (Grand Rapids, MI: Zondervan, 2011), Mark 6:22

Simon

40 Andrew, Simon Peter's brother, was one of the two who heard what John had said and who had followed Jesus. 41 The first thing Andrew did was to find his brother Simon and tell him, "We have found the Messiah" (that is, the Christ). 42 And he brought him to Jesus. *The New International Version* (Grand Rapids, MI: Zondervan, 2011), Jn 1:40–42.

Simon The Zealot

those he wanted, and they came to him. 14 He appointed twelve that they might be with him and that he might send them out to preach 15 and to have authority to drive out demons. 16 These are the twelve he appointed: Simon (to whom he gave the name Peter), 17 James son of Zebedee and his brother John (to them he gave the name Boanerges, which means "sons of thunder"), 18 Andrew, Philip, Bartholomew, Matthew, Thomas, James son of Alphaeus, Thaddaeus, Simon the Zealot 19 and Judas Iscariot, who betrayed him *The New International Version* (Grand Rapids, MI: Zondervan, 2011), Mk 3:13–19.

Simon's Wife (Eden)

14 When Jesus came into Peter's house, he saw Peter's mother-in-law lying in bed with a fever. 15 He touched her hand and the fever left her, and she got up and began to wait on him. *The New International Version* (Grand Rapids, MI: Zondervan, 2011), Mt 8:14–15.

5 Don't we have the right to take a believing wife along with us, as do the other apostles and the Lord's brothers and Cephas? *The New International Version* (Grand Rapids, MI: Zondervan, 2011), 1 Co 9:5.

Thaddaeus

2 These are the names of the twelve apostles: first, Simon (who is called Peter) and his brother Andrew; James son of Zebedee, and his brother John; 3 Philip and Bartholomew; Thomas and Matthew the tax collector; James son of Alphaeus, and Thaddaeus; 4 Simon the Zealot and Judas Iscariot, who betrayed him. *The New International Version* (Grand Rapids, MI: Zondervan, 2011) Matthew 10:2-4

The Man With Leprosy

2 A man with leprosy came and knelt before him and said, "Lord, if you are willing, you can make me clean." *The New International Version* (Grand Rapids, MI: Zondervan, 2011), Mt 8:1–2.

The Man With The Shriveled Hand (Elam)

Then Jesus said to them, "The Son of Man is Lord of the Sabbath." 6 On another Sabbath he went into the synagogue and was teaching, and a man was there whose right hand was shriveled. 7 The Pharisees and the teachers of the law were looking for a reason to accuse Jesus, so they watched him closely to see if he would heal on the Sabbath. 8 But Jesus knew what they were thinking and said to the man with the shriveled hand, "Get up and stand in front of everyone." So he got up and stood there. 9 Then Jesus said to them, "I ask you, which is lawful on the Sabbath: to do good or to do evil, to save life or to destroy it?" 10 He looked around at them all, and then said to the man, "Stretch out your hand." He did so, and his hand was completely restored. 11 But the Pharisees and the teachers of the *The New International Version* (Grand Rapids, MI: Zondervan, 2011), Lk 6:5–11.

The Men Bringing In The Paralyzed Man and The Paralyzed Man

Some men came, bringing to him a paralyzed man, carried by four of them. 4 Since they could not get him to Jesus because of the crowd, they made an opening in the roof above Jesus by digging through it and then lowered the mat the man was lying on. *The New International Version* (Grand Rapids, MI: Zondervan, 2011), Mk 2:3–4.

The Woman At The Well

28 Then, leaving her water jar, the woman went back to the town and said to the people, 29 "Come, see a man who told me everything I ever did. Could this be the Messiah?" 30 They came out of the town and made their way toward him. *The New International Version* (Grand Rapids, MI: Zondervan, 2011), Jn 4:28–30.

The Woman Healed With Issue Of Blood (Veronica)

A large crowd followed and pressed around him. 25 And a woman was there who had been subject to bleeding for twelve years. 26 She had suffered a great deal under the care of many doctors and had spent all she had, yet instead of getting better she grew worse. 27 When she heard about Jesus, she came up behind him in the crowd and touched his cloak, 28 because she thought, "If I just touch his clothes, I will be healed." 29 Immediately her bleeding stopped and she felt in her body that she was freed from her suffering. *The New International Version* (Grand Rapids, MI: Zondervan, 2011), Mk 5:24–29.

Thomas

24 Now Thomas (also known as Didymus), one of the Twelve, was not with the disciples when Jesus came. 25 So the other disciples told him, "We have seen the Lord!" But he said to them, "Unless I see the nail marks in his hands and put my finger where the nails were, and put my hand into his side, I will not believe." *The New International Version* (Grand Rapids, MI: Zondervan, 2011), Jn 20:24–25

Zebedee

19 When he had gone a little farther, he saw James son of Zebedee and his brother John in a boat, preparing their nets. 20 Without delay he called them, and they left their father Zebedee in the boat with the hired men and followed him. *The New International Version* (Grand Rapids, MI: Zondervan, 2011) Mark 1:19-20

Zechariah

18 Zechariah asked the angel, "How can I be sure of this? I am an old man and my wife is well along in years." 19 The angel said to him, "I am Gabriel. I stand in the presence of God, and I have been sent to speak to you and to tell you this good news. 20 And now you will be silent and not able to speak until the day this happens, because you did not believe my words, which will come true at their appointed time." *The New International Version* (Grand Rapids, MI: Zondervan, 2011), Luke 1:18-20

1 RESOURCES FOR EPISODE 1

Main Characters:

Mary—The mother of Jesus is visiting with her relatives, Zechariah and Elizabeth to share the good news of the future of their coming babies.

Elizabeth & Zechariah—The parents of John the Baptist who present their baby John for dedication to the priest.

Salome—The daughter of Queen Herodias who does a dance to gain the favor of her step father, Herod.

Queen Herodias—The woman who wants to have John the Baptist killed because he condemned her marriage to her brother-in-law Herod.

Zebedee, James, John—Followers of Jesus who are attempting to get a contract for selling anointing oil to synagogues.

Rhema—A follower of Christ who has returned to the group with the hope of marrying the disciple Thomas

Jairus—The chief administrator of the synagogue in Capernaum and follower of Jesus since Jesus raised his daughter from the dead.

Joanna—The wife of Chuza, and a strong supporter of John the Baptist and follower of Jesus.

John the Baptist—The one who prepared the way for Jesus to preach the kingdom of God and who is in prison facing execution.

Herod—The king who gives the order for John to be executed.

Thomas—The disciple who is planning to marry Rhema.

Andrew—The disciple of Jesus who had previously followed John and had a close relationship to him.

Jesus—The Son of God who feels the pain of losing John the Baptist and who talks about showing grief.

Summary Of Season 4 Episode 1

The scene opens with Mary, traveling to visit her relatives Zechariah and Elizabeth. A man and his wife have been hired to transport Mary from her home in Nazareth to a small town in the hill country of Judea. The wife speculates that Mary is probably pregnant and the family is sending her away in order to have the baby. The husband is not interested in the discussion and is only concerned with the reality they are being paid to do a job.

Mary is greeted at the door by Zechariah, and the moment Elizabeth hears her voice, the baby inside of her leaps in her womb. It is important to know that Zechariah and Elizabeth had been childless throughout their marriage and well along in years. One day while Zechariah was in the temple, an angel appeared to him and told him that he and Elizabeth was going to have a son. Their son would prepare the people's heart for the coming of the Messiah. His mission would be to prepare the way for the Lord to be introduced to the people of Israel. The child's name would be John and he would be great in the sight of the Lord. Zechariah did not believe the angel's words because he and Elizabeth were too old to have children. The angel told Zechariah; he would not be able to speak until after the child was born.

Mary and Elizabeth sit and talk together trying to piece together the roles their sons would have in the future kingdom of God. Elizabeth is six months pregnant, and Mary is very early in her pregnancy. An angel had informed Mary earlier that she would become pregnant by the Holy Spirit and her son would be called Jesus, and that he would be great and called the Son of the Most High. The angel also told Mary about Elizabeth's pregnancy. Unlike Zechariah, Mary immediately believed what the angel had spoken to her was true.

Elizabeth and Mary are both excited, knowing their sons' lives would be forever intertwined with each other. Not only were the boys natural relatives to each other, they would support each other in God's plan of salvation for the world.

The scene then shifts to a dance lesson being given to a young woman by the name of Salome. Salome is the daughter of Herodias. John the Baptist had publicly criticized her husband Herod for marrying her. Herodias had been the wife of Herod's brother Phillip. John considered the marriage incestuous and stating publicly that Herod's marriage to Herodias was unlawful. Herodias wanted to have John killed but Herod was against it. He believed John to be a prophet, and he feared that the people might riot if John was killed. Herod was content with locking John the Baptist up in prison, but Herodias was not. Herodias has a plan to use her daughter to get what she wanted from her husband Herod.

The scene shifts to Zebedee, James and John as they are preparing to go and sell some olive oil for the first time to make some money for the ministry. Rhema also returns to Capernaum. She had been away trying to convince her father, Khofi, to give his approval to her marrying Thomas. Khofi distrusted Jesus and had said he would never give his approval to her marrying Thomas or to the two of them leaving their jobs to follow Jesus. Barnabus and Shula arrive to greet Rhema.

The scene shifts to Joanna and her husband Chuza. Joanna had helped to support the ministry of Jesus financially earlier. Since her husband worked in Herod's household, she was able to see John the Baptist in prison by bribing the guards. She and her husband are having marital problems because of his adulteries. He knows that something is being planned for the party Herod is giving and he tries to ask her to behave at the party. The stage for the party is being built outside their window. He knows she respects John the Baptist, but he also knows of a plot Herodias has to have John killed.

The scene shifts to Simon the Zealot (Z) and Judas Iscariot washing their clothes. This is Judas's first time at manual labor. Judas is convinced it would be better if Jesus thought better when it came to money. Judas can think of several ways from his past that could be used to make money and to pay people for doing mundane chores so that the disciples and Jesus could do real ministry. Simon tries to point out that Jesus wants the disciples to relate to the people by doing the same things they do. Simon stresses that the people's perceptions were important, but Judas thinks they should follow his plan, and deal with perceptions letter. Simon stresses that Judas has plenty of knowledge, but lacks wisdom. Judas is hearing Jesus' words but is not allowing them to take root. Judas questions whether or not one can completely escape the way of thinking they had before they chose to follow Jesus.

The scene switches to the men and Tamar taking the oil to the synagogue to see if they can get a contract to sell it. One of the Pharisees refuses to allow Tamar to come into the synagogue. She is the one who came up with the formula. She starts to protest, but Zebedee silences her and James agrees to stand outside with her.

Jairus, the synagogue administrator whose daughter had been raised from the dead immediately recognized James and John and wanted to give them the contract. Rabbi Joseph who is also leaning toward following Jesus wants them to have the contract. One rabbi strongly objects, but Jairus makes the final decision to give them the contract to supply the oil.

Joanna makes an attempt to go and see John the Baptist in prison. This time the guard is unwilling to accept the bribe to allow him to see her. Orders have been given to move John from the deep prison to the room nearer the palace. This usually means a prisoner is either going to be set free or executed. By giving the guard all her money the money, the guard reveals the order to move John came from Herod. Joanna knows that John's fate is sealed. Joanna makes the decision to ride by night in a carriage to Capernaum to let Andrew and Phillip know John's fate.

When John is being moved, he is quoting from Isaiah saying the blind see, the lame walk, and the prisoners are set free etc. These were the words Jesus had sent to him when John sent his disciples to ask Jesus if he truly was the one who was to come. John was reminding himself that he had done the work he had been called to do. Thomas is excited at the prospect, but they will need Jesus' approval.

At the banquet, Herod has all of his high officials present. When Salome does her dance, Herod is greatly impressed and offers to give her whatever she wants up to half her kingdom. Herodias is now able to spring her trap. She knows Herod can't back out of his offer. She has her daughter to ask for the head of John the Baptist on a silver platter. Herod is surprised by her request, but knows his hands are tied.

The scene then takes a flashback to when John the Baptist was being brought to the priest for his dedication as a baby. Then it flashes forward to John the Baptist peacefully going to have his head cut off. It switches to Jesus as though he intuitively knows what John is currently experiencing. John mentions that he's never been to a wedding banquet, but he will be on his way to one soon. The scene goes to Joanna rushing to Capernaum and then back to John's dedication and his mission. Abner arrives to tell Jesus the news about John.

The scene goes to the priest asking what the baby's name will be. After Zechariah writes on a tablet, "His name is John," he is able to begin speaking again. As John looks out the window before his head is cut off, he sees a lamb in the field. He remembers his words about Jesus, "Behold the lamb of God, who takes away the sins of the world."

The disciples are waiting for James and John to return with news on whether or not they got the account for the olive oil. They are also congratulating Thomas and Rhema on their upcoming marriage.

They see Joanna get out of the carriage and run to Andrew's house. Andrew collapses at the news of John's death. They all run over to comfort him. Jesus also appears on the scene. Jesus has a dream of seeing John in a valley walking toward him with chains. The chains fall off and John points his arm out as though he was saying, the world is ready for you to do what you must do. Andrew and Jesus talk about the relationship between laughter and grief at the time of death. They laugh over some stale bread Jesus is trying to eat as they talk about the death of John the Baptist. Jesus emphasizes, there is no right or wrong way to grieve. Jesus asks Andrew to gather the others so they can go on a trip to honor the memory of John.

Scriptures Woven Into Season 4 Episode 1

[8] Once when Zechariah's division was on duty and he was serving as priest before God, [9] he was chosen by lot, according to the custom of the priesthood, to go into the temple of the Lord and burn incense. [10] And when the time for the burning of incense came, all the assembled worshipers were praying outside.[11] Then an angel of the Lord appeared to him, standing at the right side of the altar of incense. [12] When Zechariah saw him, he was startled and was gripped with fear. [13] But the angel said to him: "Do not be afraid, Zechariah; your prayer has been heard. Your wife Elizabeth will bear you a son, and you are to call him John.[14] He will be a joy and delight to you, and many will rejoice because of his birth, [15] for he will be great in the sight of the Lord. He is never to take wine or other fermented drink, and he will be filled with the Holy Spirit even before he is born. [16] He will bring back many of the people of Israel to the Lord their God. [17] And he will go on before the Lord, in the spirit and power of Elijah, to turn the hearts of the parents to their children and the disobedient to the wisdom of the righteous—to make ready a people prepared for the Lord." [18] Zechariah asked the angel, "How can I be sure of this? I am an old man and my wife is well along in years." [19] The angel said to him, "I am Gabriel. I stand in the presence of God, and I have been sent to speak to you and to tell you this good news. [20] And now you will be silent and not able to speak until the day this happens, because you did not believe my words, which will come true at their appointed time." **Luke 1:8-20 (NIV2011)**

[39] At that time Mary got ready and hurried to a town in the hill country of Judea, [40] where she entered Zechariah's home and greeted Elizabeth. [41] When Elizabeth heard Mary's greeting, the baby leaped in her womb, and Elizabeth was filled with the Holy Spirit. [42] In a loud voice she exclaimed: "Blessed are you among women, and blessed is the child you will bear! **Luke 1:39-42 (NIV2011)**

[1] At that time Herod the tetrarch heard the reports about Jesus, [2] and he said to his attendants, "This is John the Baptist; he has risen from the dead! That is why miraculous powers are at work in him." [3] Now Herod had arrested John and bound him and put him in prison because of Herodias, his brother Philip's wife, [4] for John had been saying to him: "It is not lawful for you to have her." [5] Herod wanted to kill John, but he was afraid of the people, because they considered John a prophet. [6] On Herod's birthday the daughter of Herodias danced for the guests and pleased Herod so much [7] that he promised with an oath to give her whatever she asked. [8] Prompted by her mother, she said, "Give me here on a platter the head of John the Baptist." [9] The king was distressed, but because of his oaths and his dinner guests, he ordered that her request be granted [10] and had John beheaded in the prison. [11] His head was brought in on a platter and given to the girl, who carried it to her mother. [12] John's disciples came and took his body and buried it. Then they went and told Jesus. **Matthew 14:1-12 (NIV2011)**

[3] Joanna the wife of Chuza, the manager of Herod's household; Susanna; and many others. These women were helping to support them out of their own means. **Luke 8:3 (NIV2011)**

[2] When John, who was in prison, heard about the deeds of the Messiah, he sent his disciples [3] to ask him, "Are you the one who is to come, or should we expect someone else?" [4] Jesus replied, "Go back and report to John what you hear and see: [5] The blind receive sight, the lame walk, those who have leprosy are cleansed, the deaf hear, the dead are raised, and the good news is proclaimed to the poor. [6] Blessed is anyone who does not stumble on account of me." **Matthew 11:2-6 (NIV2011)**

[29] Mary was greatly troubled at his words and wondered what kind of greeting this might be. [30] But the angel said to her, "Do not be afraid, Mary; you have found favor with God. [31] You will conceive and give birth to a son, and you are to call him Jesus. [32] He will be great and will be called the Son of the Most High. The

Lord God will give him the throne of his father David, [33] and he will reign over Jacob's descendants forever; his kingdom will never end." [34] "How will this be," Mary asked the angel, "since I am a virgin?" [35] The angel answered, "The Holy Spirit will come on you, and the power of the Most High will overshadow you. So the holy one to be born will be called the Son of God. [36] Even Elizabeth your relative is going to have a child in her old age, and she who was said to be unable to conceive is in her sixth month. [37] For no word from God will ever fail." **Luke 1:29-37 (NIV2011)**

[57] When it was time for Elizabeth to have her baby, she gave birth to a son. [58] Her neighbors and relatives heard that the Lord had shown her great mercy, and they shared her joy. [59] On the eighth day they came to circumcise the child, and they were going to name him after his father Zechariah, [60] but his mother spoke up and said, "No! He is to be called John." [61] They said to her, "There is no one among your relatives who has that name." [62] Then they made signs to his father, to find out what he would like to name the child. [63] He asked for a writing tablet, and to everyone's astonishment he wrote, "His name is John." [64] Immediately his mouth was opened and his tongue set free, and he began to speak, praising God. **Luke 1:57-64 (NIV2011)**

[76] And you, my child, will be called a prophet of the Most High; for you will go on before the Lord to prepare the way for him, [77] to give his people the knowledge of salvation through the forgiveness of their sins, [78] because of the tender mercy of our God, by which the rising sun will come to us from heaven [79] to shine on those living in darkness and in the shadow of death, to guide our feet into the path of peace." [80] And the child grew and became strong in spirit; and he lived in the wilderness until he appeared publicly to Israel. **Luke 1:76-80 (NIV2011)**

[23] John replied in the words of Isaiah the prophet, "I am the voice of one calling in the wilderness, 'Make straight the way for the Lord.' " **John 1:23 (NIV2011)**

[29] The next day John saw Jesus coming toward him and said, "Look, the Lamb of God, who takes away the sin of the world! [30]

This is the one I meant when I said, 'A man who comes after me has surpassed me because he was before me.' John 1:29-30 (NIV2011)

[35] The next day John was there again with two of his disciples. [36] When he saw Jesus passing by, he said, "Look, the Lamb of God!" [37] When the two disciples heard him say this, they followed Jesus. [38] Turning around, Jesus saw them following and asked, "What do you want?" They said, "Rabbi" (which means "Teacher"), "where are you staying?" [39] "Come," he replied, "and you will see." So they went and saw where he was staying, and they spent that day with him. It was about four in the afternoon. [40] Andrew, Simon Peter's brother, was one of the two who heard what John had said and who had followed Jesus. **John 1:35-40 (NIV2011)**

Biblical Characters Who Are A Part Of Season 4 Episode 1.

Mary

Mary is an actual biblical character. The role she plays in this episode with Elizabeth is entirely biblically accurate. The only deviation from Scripture is how she traveled to Elizabeth's city. The Scriptures do not mention if someone was paid to transport her from Nazareth to the hill country of Judea.

Elizabeth and Zechariah

Elizabeth and Zechariah are biblical characters. Most of the role they play are biblical accurate. The Scriptures do not mention if Zechariah was home at the time that Mary arrived. The other events surrounding them both are faithful to the texts.

John the Baptist

John the Baptist is an actual biblical character. Scriptures record that he did speak against the marriage of Herod and Herodias, and that he was executed after the dance performed by Salome at Herod's banquet. The scenes of John in prison and the words that he spoke are not found in the Scriptures, but the author uses them for literary purposes.

Salome

Salome is an actual biblical character. Although the Scriptures do no mention her dance lessons, she does do a dance that pleases Herod and leads to the execution of John the Baptist. Her name is not mentioned in the biblical texts, but she is identified by name by the historian Josephus.

Herodias

Herodias is an actual biblical character. The Scriptures do not mention any of the conversations she has in the episode, but the episode portrays her actual hatred for John the Baptist and her role in having him executed.

Zebedee, James, and John

Zebedee, James and John are actual biblical characters, however the roles they are playing in this episode concerning selling olive oil are not part of the Scriptures. The authors have woven in this story into the episodes for literary purposes.

Jairus

Jairus is a biblical character. However beyond the story of him being a synagogue ruler and the father of the girl raised from the dead, the author is using his role for literary purposes.

Joanna and Chuza,

Joanna and Chuza are both mentioned in the bible. The story surrounding them in this episode is not in the Bible, and the author is using them for literary purposes.

Herod

Herod is a biblical character. The role played by Herod in this episode is biblically accurate and found in the Scriptures.

Simon the Zealot and Judas Iscariot

Simon the Zealot and Judas Iscariot are both biblical characters, but their conversation in this episode is not found in the Scriptures. The author appears to be laying a foundation for actions that will take place in the future.

Thomas

Thomas is a biblical character and follower of Jesus. The story surrounding him and Rhema is not found in the Scriptures, and the author is using the story for literary purposes.

Andrew

Andrew is a biblical character. He was a follower of John the Baptist before following Jesus, so it is possible that he had a closer relationship to John the Baptist than the others did. The story of Joana coming to him with the news is not in the Scriptures and is done for literary purposes.

The Disciples

The Disciples are biblical characters. The roles they play concerning the sale of the olive oil and the upcoming wedding of Thomas and Rhema are not found in Scripture, and the author is using the stories for literary purposes.

Jesus

Jesus is a biblical character. The stories surrounding his reaction to John the Baptist's death and the future marriage of Thomas and Rhema are not recorded in the Scriptures. The stories are used by the author for literary purposes.

Bible Study Discussion Questions For Episode 1

1. When was a time in your life when you completed a task in your life that left you with mixed emotions when it was finally over?

2. Why do you think it was a blessing for Mary to go and talk with Elizabeth?

3. What reaction did you have to the dance performed by Salome for Herodias?

4. What do you think was at the root of Herodias' feelings toward John the Baptist?

5. Has there ever been a time when you were so angry at a person that you wanted to hurt them? How did you control yourself?

6. What strikes you about Judas in his conversation with Simon the Zealot?

7. Simon the Zealot tells Judas that Judas is smart with a lot of knowledge, but he lacks wisdom. Do you think that could be a summation of where our society is today?

8. Rhema was deeply hurt by her father's rejection of Thomas and her choice to follow Jesus. How do we disagree with a person's choices, but not destroy the relationship we have with them in the process?

9. Why do you think John the Baptist started to recite the phrases, "the blind see, the lame walk, the lepers are cleansed and the poor have the good news preached to them?"

10. What do you think was the significance of John seeing the lamb outside his window just before he was executed?

11. Do you think you could go as peacefully as John did if your life was about to be taken away from you, because of a message of truth that you preached? Would you feel as though God had let you down if God didn't stop the execution?

12. What do you think it felt like for Zechariah to get his voice back after backing up his wife's statement, "His name is John."

13. How did you feel when Andrew fell to the ground over John the Baptist's death?

14. What meaning did you get of Jesus' dream of John the Baptist walking toward Him in the open field?

15. Jesus spoke to Andrew about tears and laughter coming together at the death of a loved one? Has that been your experience in any of your losses of a loved one?

16. In what way do you find it liberating in Jesus' statement that there was no one way to experience grief?

2 Resources For Season 4 Episode 2

Main Characters

Rabbi Joseph—The rabbi who is working in conjunction with Jairus to do what he can to assist Jesus' case. He's a secret follower of Jesus.

Jairus—The synagogue administrator whose daughter Jesus raised from the dead. He's also a somewhat secret follower of Jesus because of his position.

Dominus Quintas—The Roman Official in charge of Capernaum. He wants the pilgrims who have come to see Jesus, removed from the city.

Atticus—The Roman military spy who believes that Jesus is becoming an increasing threat to Rome and wants Quintas to take action against him.

Jesus—The Son of Son leading the disciples on a road trip to teach them more about the kingdom of God.

Rhema—A follower of Jesus whose father objects to her marriage to Jesus' disciple Thomas and objects to her following Jesus. She wants Jesus to take the place of her father in giving her away in marriage.

Thomas—A disciple of Jesus who wants Jesus to give his blessing to him marrying Rhema.

Rabbi Shmuel—A Pharisee who turned in reports against Jesus, but has since had a change of heart about Jesus after Jesus invited him to pray with him at the end of Season 3. He regrets he turned John the Baptist over to the Romans.

Caiphas—The high priest who wants Jesus to be turned in to the Sanhedrin and hopes for a plot that can get Jesus arrested and executed by the Romans.

Peter—Simon has his name changed by Jesus to Peter, after Peter confesses that Jesus is the Son of the Living God. He also faces the issue of unforgiveness.

The Disciples—These are the followers of Jesus made up of men and women who travel with Jesus learning from him and doing crowd control. They also argue among themselves over Peter's new title.

Matthew—The disciple who goes to Jesus to share his hurt over Peter being elevated by Jesus. He faces the issue of needing to issue an apology and asking for forgiveness. Matthew is a friend of Gaius.

Big James and John—The two brothers and disciples of Jesus who have the most difficulty with Peter receiving the new name from Jesus.

Gaius—The Roman officer who is leaning toward believing in Jesus, but is given the order by Quintas to remove the followers of

Jesus out of the tent city located in Capernaum. He is also Matthew's former guard when Matthew was a tax collector.

Summary of Season 4 Episode 2

The scene opens with Rabbi Joseph getting dressed and reciting from the book of Ecclesiastes on all being vanity, a time and a season for everything under the sun, and the love of money. He is then counseling a young man who is dealing with a lot of anxiety. Before he finishes, Jairus the synagogue ruler appears at the door. The young man is dismissed. Rabbi Joseph asks him how things are at home, but Jairus reminds him that he is only allowed to say that his daughter was sleeping. Jairus informs Rabbi Joseph that Rabbi Shmuel is being promoted to the Sanhedrin in Jerusalem. He also lets him know that Jesus' visit to the Decapolis has resulted in additional charges being levied against him.

The scene switches to Dominus Quintas having a sculpture bust being made of him. Atticus burst into the room demanding intelligence from Quintas on Jesus and a possible uprising. Quintas assures him no uprising is on the horizon. Atticus warns him that the only reason he has his job is because his tax revenues are up higher than others, but that could change. He wants Quintas to make life difficult for followers of Jesus and to get rid of the tent city made up of pilgrims who have arrived in Capernaum. He believes Jesus may be on the verge of leading a revolution against Rome.

Jesus is leading the disciples on a road trip but the disciples have no idea where they are going. Rhema and Thomas take this as an opportunity to try and get Jesus' blessing for their marriage. Jesus' answer is somewhat disappointing when Rhema asks him to give her away in marriage. Jesus seems upset that people do not understand the reason he has come into the world. He talks about the division he has come to bring into families. His job is not to make families peaceful. He stresses that devotion to family is good only so far as it is not higher than one's devotion to God. He does give his blessing to Rhema and Thomas.

Jesus ask what gift Thomas plans to give to Rhema. Thomas tells him she does not want a gift at which point Simon interrupts him to give him a lesson on marriage. Jesus agrees with Simon giving him some advice on marriage.

The scene switches to Rabbi Shmuel getting ready of his big day of becoming a member of the Sanhedrin. In a previous episode after the feeding of the 5000, Jesus had invited Rabbi Shmuel to go and pray with him. It touched him, and he no longer saw Jesus as the threat he thought he was. Also his new position on the Sanhedrin that he had so eagerly sought after was not bringing him the joy in his life that he had suspected. The robe, the expensive perfume, the political posturing had turned him off. He realized the real reason he was being promoted was because of his earlier charges he had made against Jesus.

The scene switches to Jesus leading his followers to a pagan temple where goats are being sacrificed and other things unmentionable were being done. His followers cannot believe he has led them there.

The scene switches to the Sanhedrin in Jerusalem where Shmuel is about to receive the 70th seat in the Sanhedrin. Shmuel is shocked to learn about John the Baptist's death since he was the one that initially had him arrested by the Romans. Some members of the Sanhedrin are upset that John had been reported to the Romans without their consent. As charges are read against Jesus, many of them coming from reports by Shmuel are read, he regrets his actions even more. His day of exaltation turns into a day of regret.

There is a disagreement in the Sanhedrin over John the Baptist and Jesus. Some feel that charges against them both were biased. They wanted to hear what others had to say. Caiaphas, the high priest comes in and shuts down all debate and discussion on the matter. He wants Jesus to be reported to the Sanhedrin on his whereabouts. People are to listen closely to his teachings to try and trap him in something he might say.

The members of the Sanhedrin are also to attempt to try to get Jesus in trouble with the Romans so that Roman law can condemn him to death, and they won't have to bother with it themselves. Caiaphas orders that a decree be drawn up requiring anyone who knows the whereabouts of Jesus to report it the council immediately.

Jesus has his followers at a pagan temple. They are surprised that he would have them there when they hadn't finished the time for mourning over John. Jesus lets them know that John went to places of darkness to proclaim the kingdom of God. They must not be afraid of bringing the light into places of darkness. He poses the question to them, "Who do people say that I am?" They all give various answers, but its Simon who responds, "You are the Messiah, the Son of the Living God."

Jesus announces to Simon and to the others, that he shall no longer be called Simon, but he was changing his name to Peter. Peter means the Rock. Jesus also proclaims upon this rock I will build my church and the gates of hell shall not prevail against it. Jesus makes several statements on binding things on earth and influencing others to make the confession Peter made. Jesus talks about John the Baptist preparing the way for him.

The other followers of Jesus have a hard time with Jesus declaring that from now on, Simon will be called Peter. Jesus also explains that he wants people to follow him for the right reasons. He does not want to be perceived as a military leader seeking to overthrow Rome.

The scene shifts to the Sanhedrin with the new decree calling for Jesus and his whereabouts to be reported immediately. Rabbi Shmuel continues to regret his actions of writing the report against Jesus. He is convinced that he should be the one to find Jesus and to bring him before the Sanhedrin.

The scene shifts back to the disciples. They are arguing over Peter's new title and what the meaning of it truly is. Some are jealous. Some feel they were more deserving. Some believe Jesus knows what he's doing. Some thinks Jesus is saying Peter is saying Jesus is the best out of all the disciples.

Matthew leaves the group to have a talk with Jesus. He shares his pain that Peter was given this special title when Peter has been so mean and cruel to him. He's hurt that Jesus would give such recognition to a person who would intentionally hurt one of his own followers. Jesus surprises Matthew with the question, who was the first one to do wrong in the situation with Peter. Matthew wanted to talk about in the abstract, but Jesus had him keep in reality.

For the first time, Matthew admits all the wrong he had done to Peter that he had never apologized for. Matthew said he hadn't apologized because Peter had said he would never forgive him. Jesus pointed out an apology is a sign of repentance. Forgiveness is a gift that may or not be freely given. Meanwhile Peter is giving out instructions for the other disciples on setting up camp and sleeping arrangements for the night. They are following his instructions well.

Matthew knows he has to go to Peter and apologize. He thought by not apologizing he had been keeping the peace in the group. Jesus points out that there is no peace where two of his followers are holding resentment against each other. The following day Jesus buys nuts for the disciples as they walk along the road. He signals to Matthew during the walk that now would be a good time to go and apologize. He goes to Peter and apologizes. He asks for forgiveness, but the event does not go well. He feels even worse.

Peter has to remind others that his name is no longer Simon, but Peter. Some of them resent being reminded. Meanwhile the decree reaches Capernaum that Jesus is to be reported immediately to the Sanhedrin. Jairus informs Rabbi Joseph of the decree. Rabbi Joseph makes plans to leave Capernaum and go to Jerusalem. He is hoping with his father's influence in Jerusalem, he may be able to get a seat in the Sanhedrin to be a voice for Jesus.

The scene shifts to the bedroom of Peter and Eden. She is excited about her husband's new name. Peter is unable to fall asleep. He goes to find Jesus. He complains to Jesus about all the wrong Matthew had done to him. Jesus tells Peter to give with perfection which means forgiving 70 times 7. Peter insists that he cannot forgive him. Jesus takes Peter back to the day they first met each other. What a difference took place in him after the sun rose. Jesus acknowledges things are hard, but that people make it even harder when they lean on their own understanding.

The scene shifts to Quintas demanding that Gaius take action to begin removing the pilgrims. He gives Gaius a week to have the tent city in Capernaum destroyed. He knows the people are not leaving because they want to hear more from Jesus. He's not sure what to do. He runs into Matthew as he's leaving Quintas's office. Matthew knows Gaius is distraught and invites him to come follow Jesus and listen to his next sermon. Gaius warns Matthew to keep Jesus out of the public eyes.

The scene shifts to the women preparing to go to the Olive fields. The guys want to take Thomas into town to buy Rhema a gift for the wedding. The disciples are all around when Peter comes onto the scene and marches straight to Matthew. He puts his arms around him in a big hug and tells Matthew, I forgive you. The disciples are all in shock. Peter senses their reactions and boldly declares to everyone. It's over, it's over. I'm sorry. Matthew is left in tears.

Scriptures Woven Into Season 4 Episode 2

Vanity of vanities, saith the Preacher, vanity of vanities; all *is* vanity. **Ecclesiastes 1:2 (KJV)**

[1] To every *thing there is* a season, and a time to every purpose under the heaven: [2] A time to be born, and a time to die; a time to plant, and a time to pluck up *that which is* planted; [3] A time to kill, and a time to heal; a time to break down, and a time to build up; **Ecclesiastes 3:1-3 (KJV)**

[10] Whoever loves money never has money enough; whoever loves wealth is never satisfied with his income. This too is meaningless. **Ecclesiastes 5:10 (NIV)**

[51] Do you think I came to bring peace on earth? No, I tell you, but division. [52] From now on there will be five in one family divided against each other, three against two and two against three. [53] They will be divided, father against son and son against father, mother against daughter and daughter against mother, mother-in-law against daughter-in-law and daughter-in-law against mother-in-law." **Luke 12:51-53 (NIV)**

[27] Jesus and his disciples went on to the villages around Caesarea Philippi. On the way he asked them, "Who do people say I am?" [28] They replied, "Some say John the Baptist; others say Elijah; and still others, one of the prophets." [29] "But what about you?" he asked. "Who do you say I am?" Peter answered, "You are the Christ." **Mark 8:27-29 (NIV)**

[16] Simon Peter answered, "You are the Christ, the Son of the living God." [17] Jesus replied, "Blessed are you, Simon son of Jonah, for this was not revealed to you by man, but by my Father in heaven. [18] And I tell you that you are Peter, and on this rock I will build my church, and the gates of Hades will not overcome it. [19] I will give you the keys of the kingdom of heaven; whatever you bind on earth will be bound in heaven, and whatever you loose on earth will be loosed in heaven." [20] Then he warned his disciples not to tell anyone that he was the Christ. **Matthew 16:16-20 (NIV)**

[46] An argument started among the disciples as to which of them would be the greatest. [47] Jesus, knowing their thoughts, took a little child and had him stand beside him. [48] Then he said to them, "Whoever welcomes this little child in my name welcomes me; and whoever welcomes me welcomes the one who sent me. For it is the one who is least among you all who is the greatest." **Luke 9:46-48 (NIV)**

[45] When the chief priests and the Pharisees heard Jesus' parables, they knew he was talking about them. [46] They looked for a way to arrest him, but they were afraid of the crowd because the people held that he was a prophet. **Matthew 21:45-46**

Then the chief priests, the teachers of the law and the elders looked for a way to arrest him because they knew he had spoken the parable against them. But they were afraid of the crowd; so they left him and went away. **Mark 12:12 (NIV)**

[57] But the chief priests and the Pharisees had given orders that anyone who found out where Jesus was should report it so that they might arrest him. **John 11:57 (NIV)**

[42] Yet at the same time many even among the leaders believed in him. But because of the Pharisees they would not openly acknowledge their faith for fear they would be put out of the synagogue; [43] for they loved human praise more than praise from God. **John 12:42 (NIV)**

²¹ Then Peter came to Jesus and asked, "Lord, how many times shall I forgive my brother when he sins against me? Up to seven times?" ²² Jesus answered, "I tell you, not seven times, but seventy-seven times. **Matthew 18:21-22 (NIV)**

Biblical Characters Who Are A Part of Season 2 Episode 4

Jairus

Jairus is a biblical character, but the role he plays in this episode is not found in Scripture and is done for literary purposes.

Thomas

Thomas is one of Jesus' disciples but the role he plays in this episode preparing for his marriage is not fond in Scripture and is done for literary purposes.

The Disciples

The followers of Jesus do travel with Jesus. The Scriptures do not record Jesus and the disciples visiting a pagan temple as background for Jesus' teachings. The disciples do have an argument among themselves as to which of them might be the greatest, but the Scriptures record that argument earlier in Jesus' ministry before Simon's name is changed to Peter.

The Sanhedrin

The Sanhedrin is found in the Scriptures. The Scripture does not mention a detailed meeting of the Sanhedrin around Jesus, however the Scripture does show that the religious leaders were divided in what they thought about Jesus. The religious leaders did give orders on different occasions to either arrest Jesus or to try to trap him in what he said. The Scriptures do not record anything about Rabbi Shmuel being promoted to the 70th seat of the Sanhedrin. The story with Rabbi Shmuel is done for literary purposes.

Caiaphas

Caiaphas is found in the Scriptures as the high priest. The Scriptures do not record Caiaphas speaking at the Sanhedrin, however based on later texts closer to the arrest of Jesus before the crucifixion it is obvious that such a meeting took place.

Peter

Peter is found in Scripture and had his name changed by Jesus. He does make the confession of Jesus being the "Son of the Living God." The Scripture does not record the conflict between Matthew and Peter and does not record Jesus talking to Peter about forgiveness. The author provides the conflict for literary purposes.

Matthew

Matthew is found in Scripture, but the Scriptures do not record the conflict between him and Peter nor his relationship to Gaius. The author provides these things for literary purposes.

Jesus

The Scriptures do not record Jesus visiting the pagan temple. Jesus does however changes Simon's name to Peter. He does talk about forgiving seventy times seven though it is in a different setting. He does speak of building his church and the gates of hell not prevailing against it. He does speak of coming to bring division. Much of what he says are quotes verses from Scripture. His role with Thomas and Rhema is for literary purposes. His private talks with Peter and Matthew are done for literary purposes, but they do emphasize the teachings of Jesus.

Bible Study Discussion Questions Season 4 Episode 2

1. Is it easier for you to apologize to someone or to forgive someone? Why?

2. Has Jesus ever caused a division in your family or in a close relationship you had with another person? What turmoil do you think Rhema was experiencing with her father?

3. Do you think it was wise for Peter to instruct Thomas on getting Rhema a gift even though she said it was not necessary? Why or why not?

4. Rabbi Shmuel had always wanted to be a member of a Sanhedrin. Why is his dream come true job turning into a nightmare for him?

5. Have you ever really wanted something, but after you received it, you discovered it did not fulfill you in the way you had thought it would?

6. Why do you think Rabbi Shmuel wants to be the one to bring Jesus to the Sanhedrin?

7. Why do you think it was hard for the disciples to accept Jesus' declaration that Simon's name had been changed to Peter, The Rock?

8. What would you have felt, if you had called Peter Simon, and he corrected you and said, "my name is Peter."

9. Why do believers in Christ today have a difficult time with some believers receiving special recognition?

10. Matthew said he didn't apologize to Peter because 1) Peter had said he would never forgive him, and 2) he didn't want to disturb the peace. Do you think either of these reasons were justifiable? Which would you be more likely to use?

11. What did you think of Jesus's statement: "An apology is a sign of repentance. Forgiveness is a gift to be given or not given by the person wrong"?

12. Jesus gave Matthew the signal to go and talk with Peter on the trail. Do you think his attempt at reconciliation was a total failure? Why or why not?

13. Have you ever gone to someone thinking it was God leading you to do so, but it didn't go as plan? How did you feel afterwards?

14. Who do people say that Jesus is today?

15. Why do you think Gaius seems so confused?

16. How did you feel when Peter went and hugged Matthew and then declared to the others, "It's over"?

3 Resources For Season 4 Episode Three

Main Characters

David & Bathsheba—King David and Bathsheba are praying for their child to live however according to the prophecy of Nathan, the child dies.

Dominus Quintas—The Roman official over Capernaum whose taxes are behind and he wants the tent city in Capernaum removed because the newly arrived followers of Jesus aren't paying their share of taxes.

Gaius—The Roman official promoted by Dominus Quintas who has very mixed feelings about Jesus of Nazareth. He is going through a personal family crisis at home because one of his sons is dying with no hope of receiving medical attention.

Zebedee and Salome—They are parents of the disciples, Big James and John. They think Jesus should have given their sons special roles in the coming kingdom.

Big James & John—They are disciples of Jesus and they want to ask for special assignments in Jesus' kingdom since Jesus titled Simon, "Peter, The Rock."

Thomas & Rhema—They are followers of Jesus and are planning their wedding. They are chaperoned by various people whenever they meet alone.

Mary Magdalene—Mary is one of Jesus' followers and she prepares a large meal for him so that he will be ready physically for his next sermon.

Matthew & Peter—They are two of Jesus' disciples who are beginning a new relationship after having been reconciled to each other in the previous episode.

Barnabus and Shula—They are two friends of Jesus who were both healed by Jesus in previous episodes, and they introduce Jesus to the man born blind.

Uzziah—The name given to the man Jesus healed on the Sabbath by placing mud on his eyes. Uzziah had been born blind.

Jesus—The Messiah who heals the man born blind on the Sabbath, confronts the Pharisees with his teachings, and shares the grief with his followers.

Atticus—Roman military agent who is afraid Jesus is attempting to start a revolution against Rome, and he demands that Dominus Quintas do something to end the threat in Capernaum.

The Disciples—They are the followers of Jesus who keep trying to protect him from both the Romans and the crowds. They fear for Jesus' life more than he appears to do.

Summary of Season 4 Episode 3

The scene begins with King David lying on the floor praying and fasting. The background context is that King David had committed adultery with Bathsheba who was the wife of one of his trusted soldiers. She became pregnant, and David attempted to cover it up by sending for Uriah to come home from battle to have some time with his wife. Uriah came from the battle, but would not go home to sleep with his wife. David sent Uriah back to the battle with a note to Uriah's commander to make sure that Uriah was killed in battle.

Once Uriah was killed, David took Bathsheba as his wife. God sent Nathan the prophet to tell David that what he had done was evil in the eyes of the Lord and the child that would be born would die. After the child was born and became ill, David went into a period of fasting and praying for the child. Once the child dies, David goes to Bathsheba and tries to comfort her with the words, "the child will not come to us, but we will one day go the child."

The scene shifts to Quintas office. He is upset because his tax revenues are down. The people in tent city have been added to the tax base, but they are not paying taxes, which means Quintas may be losing his good graces with Rome. Quintas goes out and begins to physically attack some of the pilgrims. Quintas demands that Gaius shrinks the size of the tent city by 10% a day. He insults Gaius by reminding him of his Germanic background which meant he wasn't a true Roman. He also threatens to strip away his rank as a soldier.

The scene shifts to the house of Zebedee and Salome with their sons James and John. They are still having difficulty with Jesus giving Simon the name Peter meaning the rock. Salome is surprised that her sons were not given new names by Jesus after all they had worked harder than Peter. Zebedee tries to be a voice of reason but to no avail. They are surprised at the news of Peter forgiving Matthew. Salome convinces James and John that they should ask for seats of influence in Jesus's kingdom before someone else does. They are reluctant to do so because of the trouble it might cause in the group. She insists that if they will not do it, then she will do it for them.

The scene shifts to Thomas asking Rhema if she could go with him for a walk. She agrees and Andrew is assigned as their chaperone. Thomas and Rhema discuss plans for their wedding and he gives her a very special gift that has to do with time. The sundial has a very special meaning for both of them.

The scene shifts to the synagogue in Capernaum. Jairus walks in and hears the Rabbi making very condemning statements about Jesus. The Sanhedrin has identified Jesus of Nazareth as a blasphemer and a heretic. It is obvious they intend to report Jesus while he's in Capernaum.

The scene shifts to Mary Magdalene serving Jesus a big meal. She knows that Jesus is always exhausted after a sermon, so she wants to give him food to have strength to make it through. Jesus is determined to preach because of the growing tension between the Pharisees, the pilgrims, and the Romans. He feels the Pharisees have gone too far and the people are being poorly led.

The scene shifts back to James and John trying to figure out the best way to ask Jesus for their places of influence in the kingdom. It is obvious they want to be exalted higher than the others. Yet they don't want to do it in front of others.

The scene shifts to a discussion with Peter and Matthew.

Matthew is looking nervously out the window. Peter asks what's wrong and Matthew shares his concerns about the warning he had received from Gaius to keep Jesus out of the public eye. They both believe Jesus' decision to preach is a dangerous one, but they know they can't stop him.

Jesus runs into Barnabus and Shula. They tell Jesus about the latest decree coming out of Jerusalem. Jesus is to be taken into custody for blasphemy and anyone who confesses that Jesus is the Christ is to be put out of the synagogue. Jesus gets upset with the Pharisees and indicates that he will deal with the Pharisees today.

It is the Sabbath and Jesus notices a mind who has been blind since birth. He is a friend of Shula and Barnabus and his name is Uzziah and they explain his situation to Jesus. Someone asks, "who sinned, that Uzziah had been born blind." Jesus makes some mud with some spit and heals Uzziah of his blindness. A Pharisee is present at the healing and he takes Uzziah to the synagogue because the healing took place on the Sabbath.

Uzziah goes to the synagogue and is questioned by the Pharisees. His parents are also brought in for questioning about the miracle that has taken place. Uzziah, makes the statement, "whether he is a sinner or not, I do not know. One thing I know is that I was blind, and now I see." Rabbi Josiah is very angry with the man and with Jesus.

The scene goes back to Jesus teaching the crowd. The people want Jesus to do more miracles. Jesus declines. Jesus continues preaching and his message antagonizes the Pharisees. The tension starts growing. Atticus is present along with Gaius in the crowd. He demands that Gaius send a message to Quintas immediately. Gaius refuses to leave, but he does send the message to Quintas by another soldier. Quintas is informed that a mob scene is breaking out. The confrontation between Jesus and the Pharisees become more heated.

Gaius wants to keep things peaceful. He instructs a soldier not to allow any more people to reach the crowd. He calls for Matthew and tells him to get Jesus out of there.

The scene switches back to Quintas. The message that Atticus sent to him was, "what you do next will determine your career." Quintas takes off the gathering. Meanwhile the disciples are trying to get Jesus out of the area. Quintas demands that Gaius arrest Jesus, but Gaius refuses. Quintas then has Gaius arrested and he humbly accepts his fate to be arrested. Confusion takes place as the disciples are busy trying to make an escape for themselves. The Romans arrest the Pharisees that are present.

Quintas takes out his sword and demands that people tell him where Jesus is. He gets angrier and angrier that nobody will talk. Thomas in his eager desire to get Rhema to safety, runs past Quintas with his hand in Rhema's hand. In his frustration, Quintas thrust his sword through Rhema and she falls to the ground. Big James draws a knife to go an attack Quintas, but John grabs him and pulls him back. Thomas does what he can to try to help Rhema, but it is in vain. Rhema's final words to Thomas are "stay with him, that's all I want."

Although Jesus had escaped from the scene, he returned back because he felt Rhema's pain. Thomas runs to Jesus begging him to fix her and heal her because she might not be dead yet. Thomas continues to beg, but Jesus responds, "It's not her time. I love you Thomas. He loves you. I'm so sorry.

Scriptures Woven Into Season 4 Episode 3

[2] One evening David got up from his bed and walked around on the roof of the palace. From the roof he saw a woman bathing. The woman was very beautiful, [3] and David sent someone to find out about her. The man said, "Isn't this Bathsheba, the daughter of Eliam and the wife of Uriah the Hittite?" [4] Then David sent messengers to get her. She came to him, and he slept with her. (She had purified herself from her uncleanness.) Then she went back home. [5] The woman conceived and sent word to David, saying, "I am pregnant." [6] So David sent this word to Joab: "Send me Uriah the Hittite." And Joab sent him to David. [7] When Uriah came to him, David asked him how Joab was, how the soldiers were and how the war was going. [8] Then David said to Uriah, "Go down to your house and wash your feet." So Uriah left the palace, and a gift from the king was sent after him. [9] But Uriah slept at the entrance to the palace with all his master's servants and did not go down to his house. [10] When David was told, "Uriah did not go home," he asked him, "Haven't you just come from a distance? Why didn't you go home?" [11] Uriah said to David, "The ark and Israel and Judah are staying in tents, and my master Joab and my lord's men are camped in the open fields. How could I go to my house to eat and drink and lie with my wife? As surely as you live, I will not do such a thing!" [12] Then David said to him, "Stay here one more day, and tomorrow I will send you back." So Uriah remained in Jerusalem that day and the next. [13] At David's invitation, he ate and drank with him, and David made him drunk. But in the evening Uriah went out to sleep on his mat among his master's servants; he did not go home. [14] In the morning David wrote a letter to Joab and sent it with Uriah. [15] In it he wrote, "Put Uriah in the front line where the fighting is fiercest. Then withdraw from him so he will be struck down and die." [16] So while Joab had the city under siege, he put Uriah at a place where he knew the strongest defenders were. **2 Samuel 11:2-16 (NIV)**

[11] "This is what the LORD says: 'Out of your own household I am going to bring calamity upon you. Before your very eyes I will

take your wives and give them to one who is close to you, and he will lie with your wives in broad daylight. [12] You did it in secret, but I will do this thing in broad daylight before all Israel.'" [13] Then David said to Nathan, "I have sinned against the LORD." Nathan replied, "The LORD has taken away your sin. You are not going to die. [14] But because by doing this you have made the enemies of the LORD show utter contempt, the son born to you will die." [15] After Nathan had gone home, the LORD struck the child that Uriah's wife had borne to David, and he became ill. [16] David pleaded with God for the child. He fasted and went into his house and spent the nights lying on the ground. [17] The elders of his household stood beside him to get him up from the ground, but he refused, and he would not eat any food with them. [18] On the seventh day the child died. David's servants were afraid to tell him that the child was dead, for they thought, "While the child was still living, we spoke to David but he would not listen to us. How can we tell him the child is dead? He may do something desperate." [19] David noticed that his servants were whispering among themselves and he realized the child was dead. "Is the child dead?" he asked. "Yes," they replied, "he is dead." [20] Then David got up from the ground. After he had washed, put on lotions and changed his clothes, he went into the house of the LORD and worshiped. Then he went to his own house, and at his request they served him food, and he ate. [21] His servants asked him, "Why are you acting this way? While the child was alive, you fasted and wept, but now that the child is dead, you get up and eat!" [22] He answered, "While the child was still alive, I fasted and wept. I thought, 'Who knows? The LORD may be gracious to me and let the child live.' [23] But now that he is dead, why should I fast? Can I bring him back again? I will go to him, but he will not return to me." [24] Then David comforted his wife Bathsheba **2 Samuel 12:11-23 (NIV)**

[20] Then the mother of Zebedee's sons came to Jesus with her sons and, kneeling down, asked a favor of him. [21] "What is it you want?" he asked. She said, "Grant that one of these two sons of mine may sit at your right and the other at your left in your kingdom." [22] "You don't know what you are asking," Jesus said to them. "Can you drink the cup I am going to drink?" "We can," they answered. [23] Jesus said to them, "You will indeed drink from my

cup, but to sit at my right or left is not for me to grant. These places belong to those for whom they have been prepared by my Father." **Matthew 20:20-23 (NIV)**

[1] As he went along, he saw a man blind from birth. [2] His disciples asked him, "Rabbi, who sinned, this man or his parents, that he was born blind?" [3] "Neither this man nor his parents sinned," said Jesus, "but this happened so that the work of God might be displayed in his life. [4] As long as it is day, we must do the work of him who sent me. Night is coming, when no one can work. [5] While I am in the world, I am the light of the world." [6] Having said this, he spit on the ground, made some mud with the saliva, and put it on the man's eyes. [7] "Go," he told him, "wash in the Pool of Siloam" (this word means Sent). So the man went and washed, and came home seeing. **John 9:1-7 (NIV)**

[13] They brought to the Pharisees the man who had been blind. [14] Now the day on which Jesus had made the mud and opened the man's eyes was a Sabbath. [15] Therefore the Pharisees also asked him how he had received his sight. "He put mud on my eyes," the man replied, "and I washed, and now I see." [16] Some of the Pharisees said, "This man is not from God, for he does not keep the Sabbath." But others asked, "How can a sinner do such miraculous signs?" So they were divided. [17] Finally they turned again to the blind man, "What have you to say about him? It was your eyes he opened." The man replied, "He is a prophet." [18] The Jews still did not believe that he had been blind and had received his sight until they sent for the man's parents. [19] "Is this your son?" they asked. "Is this the one you say was born blind? How is it that now he can see?" [20] "We know he is our son," the parents answered, "and we know he was born blind. [21] But how he can see now, or who opened his eyes, we don't know. Ask him. He is of age; he will speak for himself." [22] His parents said this because they were afraid of the Jews, for already the Jews had decided that anyone who acknowledged that Jesus was the Christ would be put out of the synagogue. [23] That was why his parents said, "He is of age; ask him." [24] A second time they summoned the man who had been blind. "Give glory to God," they said. "We know this man is a

sinner." [25] He replied, "Whether he is a sinner or not, I don't know. One thing I do know. I was blind but now I see!" [26] Then they asked him, "What did he do to you? How did he open your eyes?" [27] He answered, "I have told you already and you did not listen. Why do you want to hear it again? Do you want to become his disciples, too?" [28] Then they hurled insults at him and said, "You are this fellow's disciple! We are disciples of Moses! [29] We know that God spoke to Moses, but as for this fellow, we don't even know where he comes from." [30] The man answered, "Now that is remarkable! You don't know where he comes from, yet he opened my eyes. [31] We know that God does not listen to sinners. He listens to the godly man who does his will. [32] Nobody has ever heard of opening the eyes of a man born blind. [33] If this man were not from God, he could do nothing." [34] To this they replied, "You were steeped in sin at birth; how dare you lecture us!" And they threw him out. **John 9:13-34 (NIV)**

[39] He answered, "A wicked and adulterous generation asks for a miraculous sign! But none will be given it except the sign of the prophet Jonah. [40] For as Jonah was three days and three nights in the belly of a huge fish, so the Son of Man will be three days and three nights in the heart of the earth. [41] The men of Nineveh will stand up at the judgment with this generation and condemn it; for they repented at the preaching of Jonah, and now one greater than Jonah is here. [42] The Queen of the South will rise at the judgment with this generation and condemn it; for she came from the ends of the earth to listen to Solomon's wisdom, and now one greater than Solomon is here. **Matthew 12:39-42 (NIV)**

[5] "Everything they do is done for men to see: They make their phylacteries wide and the tassels on their garments long; [6] they love the place of honor at banquets and the most important seats in the synagogues; [7] they love to be greeted in the marketplaces and to have men call them 'Rabbi.' **Matthew 23:5-7 (NIV)**

[23] "Woe to you, teachers of the law and Pharisees, you hypocrites! You give a tenth of your spices--mint, dill and cummin. But you

have neglected the more important matters of the law--justice, mercy and faithfulness. You should have practiced the latter, without neglecting the former. [24] You blind guides! You strain out a gnat but swallow a camel. [25] "Woe to you, teachers of the law and Pharisees, you hypocrites! You clean the outside of the cup and dish, but inside they are full of greed and self-indulgence. [26] Blind Pharisee! First clean the inside of the cup and dish, and then the outside also will be clean. [27] "Woe to you, teachers of the law and Pharisees, you hypocrites! You are like whitewashed tombs, which look beautiful on the outside but on the inside are full of dead men's bones and everything unclean. [28] In the same way, on the outside you appear to people as righteous but on the inside you are full of hypocrisy and wickedness. **Matthew 23:23-28 (NIV)**

Biblical Characters Who Are A Part Of Season 4 Episode 3

David & Bathsheba

David & Bathsheba are biblical characters and the story line in this episode is close to the Biblical account. However David is alerted to the child's death, not by Bathsheba's scream but rather because his servants are whispering to each other. Some of the words that David speaks to Bathsheba are actually spoken to his servants. The Scriptures do not record any of the words of Bathsheba, but the Scriptures do indicate that David comforted her after the death of the child.

Zebedee & Salome

Zebedee and Salome are the parents of James and John. The scriptures do not record the four of them having this conversation. The scriptures do give an account of Salome asking for special seats for her sons from Jesus. The scriptures also give an account of the two brothers asking for special seats from Jesus.

Thomas

Thomas is a disciple of Jesus, however all of the story centered around preparing to marry Rhema is an account of the author's literary purposes. Therefore, the bible does not record Thomas losing his fiancée.

Jairus

Jairus is a biblical character, however the roles he plays in this episode are done for the author's literary purposes.

Peter & Matthew

Peter and Matthew are biblical characters, however the roles they play in this episode are done for the author's literary purposes.

Jesus

Jesus does heal a man on the Sabbath who had been born blind. The Scriptures do not record Shula and Barnabus so their role is part of the author's literary purposes. The Scriptures indicate that Jesus sent the man to the Pool of Siloam to wash and be healed, whereas in this episode Jesus had him wash from a bucket. The Scriptures do record Jesus' confrontation with the Pharisees and when he does, his remarks are taken from the Scriptures. The Scriptures do not record the coming marriage of Thomas and Rhema so all of Jesus' interactions around that role are done for literary purposes.

Uzziah

The Scriptures do record Jesus healing a man born blind on the Sabbath, but the Scriptures do no give the man a name. Uzziah is used for the author's literary purposes. The encounter Uzziah later has with the Pharisees is very close to the account found in Scripture including his parents' arrival to identify him. The parents would not make a statement about Jesus or the healing method because of the threat of being put out of the synagogue.

The Disciples

The Disciples are with Jesus during the healing of the man born blind. The Scriptures indicate that they were the ones to asks, "who sinned this man or his parents" as opposed to the stranger asking the question in the episode. Since the story of Thomas and Rhema is due to the author's literary purposes, none of their reactions are found in Scripture to Rhema's death.

Bible Study Discussion Questions For Season 4 Episode 3

1. What was one major prayer you prayed that God answered with a No, and how did you feel afterwards?

2. What words would you have shared with Bathsheba before the baby died if you had known about Nathan's prophecy?

3. Do you think John and James were wrong for wanting places of influence in Jesus' kingdom? Why or why not?

4. How do we cloak our own selfish ambition in religious terms to make them sound not so selfish? What are the motives we might have for doing good things that we are not aware of at the moment?

5. Why did Jesus heal Uzziah on the Sabbath knowing it could cause problems?

6. What testimony did Uzziah seem to rely upon when it came to Jesus?

7. Why is our personal testimony something we can hold on to in the midst of a trial?

8. How did you feel toward the Pharisees as they attacked Jesus?

9. What do you think is going on inside of Gaius when he refuses to arrest Jesus knowing that it could cost him his life?

10. What feeling ran through you when Rhema had the sword pushed in and pulled out of her as she fell to the ground?

11. Big James pulled out a knife to go after Dominus. How does a believer get to the place of being willing to kill another person? Do you think you could reach that point?

12. Why do you think Rhema's last words to Thomas were "stay with Him, that's all I want"? What do her words reveal about her?

13. When have you experienced a sudden unexpected death of someone very close to you?

14. If you had of been Thomas, do you think your reaction to Rhema's death would have been different from his when Jesus arrived on the scene? Why or why not?

15. What significance if any do you find in the gift Thomas gave to Rhema had to do with time?

16. What affected you the most in this episode?

4 Season 4 Episode Four

Main Characters

Quintas—The former praetor of Capernaum who is removed from office for the murder of Rhema.

Atticus—The Roman military cohort who crowns Gaius as the new praetor over Capernaum.

Gaius –The former guard for Matthew when he was tax collector, friend of Simon because of personal family issues, new praetor of Capernaum, and the Roman whose servant/son is sick.

Thomas—The disciple of Jesus who is grieving the most over the death of Rhema, his soon to be bride.

Kofni—The father of Rhema, who objected to her following Jesus and to her marrying Thomas.

Peter—The disciple called by Jesus to take a leading role and who changed his name from Simon to Peter meaning the Rock. He became a friend of Gaius.

Peter, James & John—The three disciples who witnessed Jesus raising Jairus' daughter from the dead and were forbidden by Jesus to tell anyone what they saw.

Little James & Thaddeus—The first of the disciples to walk with Jesus in the Chosen.

Matthew—The disciple, who was a former tax collector, is called in to see Gaius.

James & John—Two brothers who were called by Jesus. Jesus gave them the name Sons of Thunder. They request special seats in Jesus' kingdom.

Jesus—The Son of God who does several miracles, but is becoming increasingly distressed over the failure of the disciples to grasp the meaning of his words.

The Disciples—Jesus followers who are around Jesus all the time, but are failing to grasp the meanings of his teachings.

Summary of Season 4 Episode 4

In episode three, Dominus Quintas was afraid of losing his job in the Roman government over a loss of tax revenue and the growing tent city which could become a center of rebellion. Atticus had believed that Gaius was attempting to sabotage Quintas so that Quintas would lose his position and Gaius would gain Quintas's seat. Atticus wanted to see Quintas removed because he was not acting quickly enough to put down a rebellion before it could get started. Atticus perceived Jesus to be a real threat to Rome's authority.

Quintas had ordered Gaius to arrest Jesus at the mob scene caused by the Pharisees reaction to Jesus' teachings, but Gaius refused. Gaius knew he was giving up everything in refusing Quintas'command. He was arrested on the spot. Quintas is very angry with all the people on the scene, because none of them would tell where Jesus was. His disciples had whisked him away down an alley. To make an example before the others, Quintas took his sword and thrust it through Rhema, causing her death.

Episode four begins with Quintas being brought in before the Roman authorities in chains. He loses his rank and position over murdering an innocent civilian. It appears Atticus has a role in this. Next Gaius is brought into the chamber in chains, expecting to be executed for disobeying a direct order. To his surprise Atticus informs him that he is the new praetor and has been assigned to replace Quintas in his former role in Capernaum.

The scene switches to Jesus and his followers on the road carrying Rhema' body back to her father Kofni for him to give her a burial in his hometown. Thomas is in tremendous grief over the death of his bride to be. Peter wants to do something but because he doesn't know what to do, he tells Jesus that he feels as though he is failing in his role as the Rock. Jesus points out that death is the way of all the earth. He further points out that Thomas does not need a rock at this point, all he needs is someone to be with him.

All of the followers are handling their grief in different ways. Mary seeks to blame herself in that if only she had paid closer attention to Rhema. Tamar insists that she not try to blame herself. The big question on their minds is, "could Jesus have stopped this?"

The scene switches to Peter, James, and John and the discussion they are having over, "If Jesus could raise Jairus daughter why not raise Rhema?" Peter reminds them that Jesus had forbidden them to talk to anyone about what happened at Jairus' home. The verse in Isaiah 55:8 comes up again and again in the episode, "For my thoughts are not your, neither are your ways my ways" declares the Lord. The three are very concerned that if Jesus should raise someone else from the dead, Jesus' actions would destroy Thomas.

There are a series of quick scene changes sort of like mini flashbacks as Jesus and the followers continue to carry Rhema's body to her family. John and James talk about having done everything together up to the point of Jesus sending them out two by two. But Jesus had paired John with Thomas. James confessed he was jealous of the closeness that developed between his brother and Thomas while they were out ministering together. He encouraged John to go and be with Thomas because of their closeness to each other. Thomas flashes back to him and Rhema talking to each other and then to seeing her die. Thomas finds comfort in the arms of Jesus and of John.

As they approach Rhema's hometown, Thomas is worried about what he will say to Rhema's father. Before they reach the town, Kofni and a group of his men are approaching from the opposite direction to take the body themselves into the town. Kofni and his group are very rude to Jesus and his followers. Kofni personally attacks Jesus with his words, accuses Thomas of murdering his daughter, and forbids them from coming any closer to his town. Jesus words to Kofni falls on deaf ears, as do the words of Thomas. Kofni vows to expose Jesus to the world as a fraud and false prophet. After Jesus and his disciples turn to leave, Kofni continues his insults until Simon the Zealot puts a stop to it. Kofni does not accept that Jesus and his followers are in mourning.

Jesus and his followers head toward Jerusalem. Money is given to Judas from the sale of the anointing oil but it's not much. Jesus passes by a man who is possessed by a demon on the roadside. He casts the demon out and the man's mind is restored.

There are a series of quick scene changes with Rabbi Joseph arriving at the Sanhedrin in Jerusalem, Thomas thinking of his grief, Jesus healing a blind man in the streets, Kofni preaching against Jesus, and Jesus preaching to his followers and others. A Roman soldier brings an order in to Gaius and he quickly burns it up.

Several months have passed since Rhema's death. Peter tries talking to Thomas about how he's now feeling inside. Peter offers Thomas some Scriptures, but Thomas does not find them very helpful. Thomas told Peter, "It is painful to be here, but there's not other place I would rather be."

Jesus and the group are all back in Capernaum at Peter and Eden's home. The disciples have a way of getting into arguments over small things and this time its over the proper way to eat pomegranates. Jesus leaves the room to go outside to be with Little James and Thaddeus. The three of the reminisce over old times. Jesus pointed out that it was a lifetime they could not go back to. Little James has a feeling that they will be leaving Capernaum because of some of the things Jesus has said would happen to him.

Andrew tells the others to get ready to leave Capernaum. Salome reminds James and John to ask for seats in the kingdom on the trip. Roman soldiers arrive to take away Matthew. Peter agrees to go with Matthew. They are brought before Gaius. Gaius warns them about edicts coming out of Jerusalem concerning Jesus. He instructs them to have Jesus take a low profile. There are people that want Jesus killed. Gaius confesses that he has become a believer in Jesus. They take Gaius to Jesus to have him ask for a healing for his servant/son. Gaius bows before Jesus and confesses his unworthiness to ask for a healing. He tells Jesus if you just say the word, my son will be healed. Jesus commends Gaius in front of all the others for his faith and grants him his healing according to his faith.

James and John make their request for seats at Jesus' right and left in the new kingdom in front of the other disciples. Jesus is deeply disturbed by their request and reminds them of the suffering he is about to endure. The other disciples get very angry with James and John over the request and jealousy erupts. Jesus teaches them what authority in his kingdom is to look like and it involves being the greatest servant. The followers do not understand Jesus saying "The Son of man came to give his life as a ransom for many.

Gaius is seen buying items from the merchants in tent city and leaving tips for the merchants. When Gaius arrives home, he is greeted by his wife with great news, but before she can say anything he says I know. There is a healing not only with his son, but with his family. Gaius teaches them what Peter taught him, shalom, shalom.

Jesus is somewhat discouraged by his followers and sends them alone towards Jerusalem and promises to catch up with them. Jesus watches Mary, Tamar, and Zebedee making olive oil, he almost begins to cry over the crushing of the grapes. Gaius appears in the background, and he and Jesus embrace each other.

Scriptures Woven Into Season 4 Episode 4

8 "For My thoughts are not your thoughts, Neither are your ways My ways," declares the LORD. **Isaiah 55:8 (NASB77)**

18 "And I also say to you that you are Peter, and upon this rock I will build My church; and the gates of Hades shall not overpower it. **Matthew 16:18 (NASB77)**

49 While He was still speaking, someone •came from the house of the synagogue official, saying, "Your daughter has died; do not trouble the Teacher anymore."50 But when Jesus heard this, He answered him, " Do not be afraid any longer; only believe, and she shall be made well."51 And when He had come to the house, He did not allow anyone to enter with Him, except Peter and John and James, and the girl's father and mother.52 Now they were all weeping and lamenting for her; but He said, "Stop weeping, for she has not died, but is asleep."53 And they began laughing at Him, knowing that she had died.54 He, however, took her by the hand and called, saying, "Child, arise!"55 And her spirit returned, and she rose immediately; and He gave orders for something to be given her to eat. 56 And her parents were amazed; but He instructed them to tell no one what had happened. **Luke 8:49-56 (NASB77)**

41 And hearing this, the ten began to feel indignant with James and John. 42 And calling them to Himself, Jesus •said to them, "You know that those who are recognized as rulers of the Gentiles lord it over them; and their great men exercise authority over them.43 "But it is not so among you, but whoever wishes to become great among you shall be your servant; 44 and whoever wishes to be first among you shall be slave of all. 45 "For even the Son of Man did not come to be served, but to serve, and to give His life a ransom for many." **Mark 10:41-45 (NASB77)**

7 And He •summoned the twelve and began to send them out in pairs; and He was giving them authority over the unclean spirits; **Mark 6:7 (NASB77)**

32 And they were on the road, going up to Jerusalem, and Jesus was walking on ahead of them; and they were amazed, and those who followed were fearful. And again He took the twelve aside and began to tell them what was going to happen to Him,33 saying, "Behold, we are going up to Jerusalem, and the Son of Man will be delivered to the chief priests and the scribes; and they will condemn Him to death, and will deliver Him to the Gentiles.34 "And they will mock Him and spit upon Him, and scourge Him, and kill Him, and three days later He will rise again." **Mark 10:32-34 (NASB77)**

24 And the news about Him went out into all Syria; and they brought to Him all who were ill, taken with various diseases and pains, demoniacs, epileptics, paralytics; and He healed them. **Matthew 4:24 (NASB77)**

24 And there arose also a dispute among them as to which one of them was regarded to be greatest. 25 And He said to them, "The kings of the Gentiles lord it over them; and those who have authority over them are called 'Benefactors.'26 "But not so with you, but let him who is the greatest among you become as the youngest, and the leader as the servant.27 "For who is greater, the one who reclines at the table, or the one who serves? Is it not the one who reclines at the table? But I am among you as the one who serves.28 "And you are those who have stood by Me in My trials;29 and just as My Father has granted Me a kingdom, I grant you 30 that you may eat and drink at My table in My kingdom, and you will sit on thrones judging the twelve tribes of Israel. **Luke 22:24-30 (NASB77)**

40 And while the sun was setting, all who had any sick with various diseases brought them to Him; and laying His hands on every one of them, He was healing them. **Luke 4:40 (NASB77)**

35 And James and John, the two sons of Zebedee, •came up to Him, saying to Him, "Teacher, we want You to do for us whatever we ask of You."36 And He said to them, "What do you want Me to do for you?" 37 And they said to Him, " Grant that we may sit in Your glory, one on Your right, and one on Your left."38 But Jesus said to them, "You do not know what you are asking for. Are you able to drink the cup that I drink, or to be baptized with the baptism with which I am baptized?"39 And they said to Him, "We are able." And Jesus said to them, "The cup that I drink you shall drink; and you shall be baptized with the baptism with which I am baptized.40 "But to sit on My right or on My left, this is not Mine to give; but it is for those for whom it has been prepared." **Mark 10:35-40** **(NASB77)**

5 And when He had entered Capernaum, a centurion came to Him, entreating Him, 6 and saying, " Lord, my servant is lying paralyzed at home, suffering great pain."7 And He •said to him, "I will come and heal him."8 But the centurion answered and said, " Lord, I am not worthy for You to come under my roof, but just say the word, and my servant will be healed.9 "For I, too, am a man under authority, with soldiers under me; and I say to this one, 'Go!' and he goes, and to another, 'Come!' and he comes, and to my slave, 'Do this!' and he does it."10 Now when Jesus heard this, He marveled, and said to those who were following, "Truly I say to you, I have not found such great faith with anyone in Israel. 11 "And I say to you, that many shall come from east and west, and recline at the table with Abraham, and Isaac, and Jacob, in the kingdom of heaven;12 but the sons of the kingdom shall be cast out into the outer darkness; in that place there shall be weeping and gnashing of teeth."13 And Jesus said to the centurion, "Go your way; let it be done to you as you have believed." And the servant was healed that very hour. **Matthew 8:5-13 (NASB77)**

The Pharisees went out and immediately *began* conspiring with the Herodians against Him, as to how they might put Him to death **Mark 3:6 (NASB77)**

--

Biblical Characters Who Are Part of Season 4 Episode 4

Peter

Peter is an actual biblical character. Jesus does give Simon the name Peter meaning the Rock. Undoubtedly Peter had struggles trying to figure out how this name should change his role among the disciples, but the Gospels do not provide us with insight on this other than Jesus telling Peter "After he had turned to strengthen his brothers". Almost all of the roles Peter has in this episode is due to the author's literary purpose of building the story that is yet to come.

The Disciples

The disciples are biblical characters. They do become upset over James and John requesting special seats in the kingdom in the Scriptures. They do listen to Jesus' teachings on what it means to be a leader in the kingdom, and they do observe Jesus's words on the faith of the Roman soldier. The Roman soldier or centurion is never named in the Scriptures although he is given the name Gaius in the episode. But all the references to their behavior and reactions concerning Rhema are not found in the Scriptures and are due to the author's literary purposes. The interactions with Gaius by Matthew and Peter are not found in the Scriptures.

Peter, James & John,

The three are biblical characters, and they were the only ones allowed to see Jesus raise Jairus's daughter from the dead according the Scriptures. The Scriptures do not record them discussing this event, and it is in the episode for the author's literary purposes.

James & John,

James and John are disciples of Jesus, they are brothers, and their parents are Zebedee and Salome. The Scriptures do record them asking Jesus for seats on his right and left side, as well as their willingness to drink from the cup he drinks. Their actions did cause resentment among the disciples. The Scriptures do not record the conversation of Jesus pairing John with Thomas. This is in the episode for the author's literary purposes.

Thomas

Thomas is one of Jesus' disciples. The Scriptures do not record anything about him preparing to marry Rhema and all the events stemming from it. This is in the episode for the author's literary purposes. The story may be present to help us understand why Thomas was the biggest doubter of Jesus' resurrection.

Jesus

Jesus is the Messiah. Scriptures record that he did cast out demons, he did heal blind people, he did teach on authority in the kingdom, he did heal a Roman centurion's servant and commend him for his faith, he did become discouraged at the disciple's lack of ability to understand his teachings, he did say he had come to give his life as a ransom for many, and he did change Simon's name to Peter. Not all of the individual healings are related to a particular verse in Scripture. Sometimes it simply says that all who came to him were healed. The Scriptures do no record any of the events involving Rhema's death, and they are present for the author's literary purposes.

Bible Study Discussion Questions For Season 4
Episode 4

1. When have you experienced a tragedy in which you thought, if you had of just done this, the situation could have been prevented? What does this kind of thinking lead to in the long run?

2. Gaius had a tremendous turn of events in his life. Have you ever had a drastic turn of events after taking a stand for your beliefs?

3. Do you think Jesus intended to place a heavy burden on Simon by changing his name to Peter? Why do we place extra pressure on ourselves when Jesus has called us to rest?

4. Peter, James and John were worried that if Jesus raised anyone else from the dead, it would destroy Thomas. Do you agree or disagree with their assessment and why?

5. Kofni rages at Jesus, Thomas, and the disciples over the death of Rhema. Do you think guilt may have played a part in his anger? Is there anything they could have said to Kofni that would have a difference?

6. Kofni accused Thomas of murdering his daughter? Have you been in that situation in which something happened which was not all your fault, but you were blamed for it? If so, how did it affect your walk with the Lord?

7. What did you learn from the way in which Peter tried to help Thomas deal with his grief?

8. The disciples were arguing over the right way to cut a pomegranate. Do you think Jesus is grieved by some of the silly arguments we have with each other? How can we prevent them?

9. What do you think drove Gaius to his belief in Jesus? What drove you to Christ?

10. Are any of us worthy for God to be obligated to do something for us? Why do we sometimes feel that way?

11. When Jesus told the disciples he had not found such great faith in all of Israel as he did in Gaius, how do you think this made the disciples feel?

12. Do you think James and John had good motives in asking Jesus for positions in the kingdom? How do we test our motives when we seek a higher role in the kingdom?

13. Do you think the disciples were justified in their anger towards James and John?

14. What do you think is the most frustrating thing for Jesus in this episode?

15. What do you think was the author's intention in including the final scene of Jesus being troubled looking at the grapes being crushed?

5 SEASON 4 EPISODE 5

Main Characters

Pharisees—The Pharisees were a prominent Jewish sect known for their strict adherence to the Torah as well as the oral traditions which they believed to complement the written law. They were influential among the common people and emphasized the importance of purity laws and the belief in the resurrection of the dead, judgment in the afterlife, and the existence of angels.

Sadducees—The Sadducees were a sect that emerged from the priestly and aristocratic classes. Unlike the Pharisees, they accepted only the written Torah as authoritative and rejected beliefs not explicitly stated therein, such as the resurrection of the dead, the afterlife, and the existence of angels. The Sadducees were known for their conservative stance and control of the Temple worship and sacrifices.

Sanhedrin—The Sanhedrin was the supreme council and court in ancient Israel, composed of 71 members, including chief priests, scribes, and elders. It had authority over religious and legal matters and could make judgments on a wide range of issues, from criminal cases to religious disputes. The Pharisees and Sadducees often had representation within the Sanhedrin, reflecting the diverse opinions and interpretations of Jewish law and tradition.

Joanna—One of the women who supported Jesus and the disciples out of her own property.

Judas—The disciple of Jesus who is responsible for handling the money and financial affairs of the group.

Rabbi Shmuel—A Pharisee from Capernaum who at first wanted to expose Jesus as a heretic, but later changed his mind about Jesus after Jesus and he prayed together in an episode in scene three. He was invited to join the Sanhedrin because of his work in exposing the actions of Jesus in regards to the Sabbath.

Rabbi Joseph—A Pharisee from Capernaum and close friend of Jairus, who goes to Jerusalem to try to protect Jesus. He receives a seat in the Sanhedrin because of his father's wealth.

The Disciples—The followers of Jesus who accompany Jesus on his travels and are the main recipients of his teachings.

Lazarus, Martha, & Mary—Friends of Jesus who live in the town of Bethany. Mary is known for listening to the words of Jesus. Martha is known for working hard doing things to serve Jesus and his followers.

Roman Soldiers—The group of Romans who force Jesus and his followers to carry their equipment for a mile, according to Roman law at that time.

Mary—Jesus' mother listens to his frustrations.

Jesus—The Messiah trying to teach his followers the ways of the kingdom of God.

Summary of Season 4 Episode 5

The episode begins with the disciples traveling on the road to Jerusalem as instructed to do so by Jesus in the previous episode. A mysterious rider approaches them to deliver a package to Andrew and Simon. They are hesitant at first to accept the package because they don't know what it might contain. Numerous predictions are given, but none are accurate. The box is a gift from Joanna, the wife of Chuza. She has sent items to be sold in order to support Jesus' ministry. Judas divides up the items among the disciples based on their knowledge of the value of the items, and Peter sends the followers of Jesus out to sell them.

The scene switches to the Sanhedrin in Jerusalem and the Pharisees and Sadducees are debating each other. The Pharisees claim there is a resurrection of the body but the Sadducees claim there is no afterlife. The Sadducees come from the wealthiest part of society. The Pharisees accuse the Sadducees of being biased in their interpretation of the Scripture by the wealth they possessed.

Rabbi Joseph from Capernaum has gained a seat in the Sanhedrin because of his father's wealth. He arrives at the Sanhedrin and is recognized by Rabbi Shmuel who was also formerly from Capernaum. Both of them are sympathetic toward Jesus for different reasons, but neither knows of the other's position toward Jesus. Rabbi Shmuel attempts to introduce Rabbi Joseph to the right people and sometimes it goes well and sometimes it does not.

The disciples want to make plans as to where they should set up camp near Jerusalem. Judas suggests they use some of their wealth from Joanna's gift and stay in hotels. Before they can settle on a place, Jesus catches up with them and informs them they will be staying in Bethany at the home of Lazarus, Mary and Martha.

As they begin their journey together, a group of Roman soldiers demand that Jesus and his followers drop their baggage, and carry the Romans gear and equipment for a mile based on Roman law. The disciples object, but Jesus encourages them to accept the task. The Romans load them down with Roman gear and insults them as they are beginning the mile long journey to the next sign post.

The scene switches back to the Sanhedrin. Rabbi Shmuel is explaining to Rabbi Joseph the background and history of the different groups in the building. He explains how things work and how a lot of people lose their zeal for making changes once they arrive in the Sanhedrin. Rabbi Shmuel continues to educate Rabbi Joseph on the groups in the Sanhedrin. He explains the difference between those who lean toward Hillel and those who lean toward Shemai. Hillel focuses in on the principle of the law, whereas Shemai leans toward a literal interpretation. For some reason, Shmuel appears troubled.

The scene goes back to Jesus and his followers coming to the end of the mile marker. The soldiers tell them to stop, but Jesus keeps going. When he's ordered to stop, he reminds the Roman soldier that the law required one mile, but there was no law against voluntarily assisting the soldiers for a second mile. The disciples reluctantly follow in Jesus' footsteps and continue on with the journey. One by one, the Roman soldiers are touched, and they begin to take back some of the load and carry it themselves. Fortunately, when Jesus' followers return to their items on the road, they are all still there.

The scene goes back to the Sanhedrin as the speaker reminds them of Pilate's illegal activities and atrocities against some of the Jews protesting his actions. Pilate's actions have gotten him into trouble with Tiberius Ceasar. The speaker says they could use

Pilate's predicament in their favor. They might even be able to take care of some things they have been putting off. Rabbi Joseph wants to speak up, but Rabbi Shmuel stops him and tells him to pick his battles well. He encourages him to join a committee and get in standing with others before speaking. Rabbi Shmuel finds it hard to direct Rabbi Joseph, because Rabbi Joseph does not tip his hand that he is there to help Jesus. He does choose the committee dealing with the fulfillment of prophecies.

The scene switches back to Jesus and the disciples on the road to Bethany. One disciple points out to Jesus that to go the extra mile actually ends up being three miles if you include the mile to go back and get your stuff. Jesus commends the followers on the extra mile because he knew how hard it was for them to do it. Judas asks Jesus for permission to visit a mentor of his after they reach Bethany. Jesus gives him permission to do so after they've had supper with Mary, Martha and Lazarus.

When they reach Bethany, Mary comes out of the house to greet them and fixes her gaze on Jesus the whole time he is in the home. Martha stays inside the house to make sure everything is nearly perfect for their arrival. Lazarus shocks the disciples by his rebuke of Jesus showing up unannounced at the house with a group of people. But it's all part of a joke between Lazarus and Jesus. Jesus and his followers are made to feel right at home. Jesus is eager to see his mother, Mary, who has moved in with Lazarus and his sisters due to the tension in Nazareth. The last time Jesus was in Nazareth, the religious leaders had attempted to throw him off a cliff. Mary is out picking berries because she knows which ones are edible.

Rabbi Shmuel continues to take Rabbi Joseph all around the Sanhedrin to introduce him to others. Often times the introductions do not go well. Some object to Rabbi Joseph getting a seat on the Sanhedrin because of his father's wealth, some object because he is a Pharisee and not a Sadducee, and some object because of his father's business dealings. Rabbi Shmuel has become very adept at handling things politically.

The scene shifts back to Jesus and the disciples at Lazarus's home. Mary is sitting listening to every word from Jesus. Martha is busy trying to prepare the food for everyone to eat. Jesus tells the story of the workers hired to go into the vineyard at different times of the day, but in the end they all receive the same pay for their labor. The disciples think the kingdom of heaven may not be fair. Jesus says the point is that people are not measured by what they deserve. The last will be first and the first will be last.

Meanwhile Martha is getting more upset that Mary has not offered to come and help her. Martha finally speaks up and blasts her sister in front of everyone for not helping her. Jesus diffuses the situation by commending Martha on the great work she has done, but points out that Mary has made the wiser choice by choosing to take in his words. The best way to serve Him is by paying close attention to his words. His words have eternal value. He does tell Mary that she could have helped out her sister a little. Lazarus volunteers to assist in serving the meal and they all have a great evening. Jesus does notice that Lazarus has some severe pains in his side that he is trying to keep hidden from the others.

Jesus gives permission to Judas to go and visit his mentor. Jesus' mother Mary shows up. They joke together and reminisce about Nazareth. Mary points out that her thoughts dwell in the land of the living. They discuss the poverty they knew when Jesus was growing up. Jesus shares some of the frustrations he's having with the disciples. It seems as though no one understands what he's been called to do. The religious leaders call his teachings blasphemy, some people take his teachings the wrong way, and though his followers agree with what he says, they act in a way as if they never heard him speak.

Judas goes to visit his old mentor and is troubled when he arrives there. Judas wants to get ready for Jesus to set up his kingdom but is worried Jesus lacks the financial resources to make it happen. His mentor is very shrewd. He convinces Judas that he should be paid for serving as treasurer and that he should set aside some of the money he's collecting for investments. He even points out that Judas will most likely be Secretary of Treasury in the new regime, so he should start making financial decisions on his own rather than waiting for permission. Judas admits to being angry and that his understanding is shaken. His mentor uses religious words to persuade Judas to handle the money in the way he thinks is best.

The scene switches back to the Sanhedrin. Rabbi Shmuel continues his introductions of Rabbi Joseph to others. They are informed by one leader of a plot to have Jesus killed by the Romans in order to bring attention to restoring the original boundaries of Israel. Some people are blaming Jesus for the death of Rhema and plan to prosecute him for it. The justification for killing Jesus is that in the long run it will help the nation. Rabbi Shmuel and Rabbi Joseph are both shocked and disturbed by the plot. They can't believe a fellow member of the Sanhedrin would try to profit off of taking a person's life for political gain.

The scene switches back to Lazarus' home as Jesus and his followers prepare to continue their journey on to Jerusalem. Judas takes his first money out of the money bag and puts it in his own pocket.

Scriptures Woven Into Season 4 Episode 5

6 Then Paul, knowing that some of them were Sadducees and the others Pharisees, called out in the Sanhedrin, "My brothers, I am a Pharisee, descended from Pharisees. I stand on trial because of the hope of the resurrection of the dead."7 When he said this, a dispute broke out between the Pharisees and the Sadducees, and the assembly was divided.8 (The Sadducees say that there is no resurrection, and that there are neither angels nor spirits, but the Pharisees believe all these things.)9 There was a great uproar, and some of the teachers of the law who were Pharisees stood up and argued vigorously. "We find nothing wrong with this man," they said. "What if a spirit or an angel has spoken to him?"**Acts 23:6-9 (NIV2011)**

3 Joanna the wife of Chuza, the manager of Herod's household; Susanna; and many others. These women were helping to support them out of their own means. **Luke 8:3 (NIV2011)**

4 But one of his disciples, Judas Iscariot, who was later to betray him, objected,5 "Why wasn't this perfume sold and the money given to the poor? It was worth a year's wages."6 He did not say this because he cared about the poor but because he was a thief; as keeper of the money bag, he used to help himself to what was put into it.7 "Leave her alone," Jesus replied. "It was intended that she should save this perfume for the day of my burial. **John 12:4-7 (NIV2011)**

38 As Jesus and his disciples were on their way, he came to a village where a woman named Martha opened her home to him.39 She had a sister called Mary, who sat at the Lord's feet listening to what he said.40 But Martha was distracted by all the preparations that had to be made. She came to him and asked, "Lord, don't you care that my sister has left me to do the work by myself? Tell her to help me!"41 "Martha, Martha," the Lord answered, "you are worried and upset about many things, 42 but few things are needed—or indeed only one. Mary has chosen what is better, and it will not be taken away from her." **Luke 10:38-42 (NIV2011)**

1 "For the kingdom of heaven is like a landowner who went out early in the morning to hire workers for his vineyard.2 He agreed to pay them a denarius for the day and sent them into his vineyard.3 "About nine in the morning he went out and saw others standing in the marketplace doing nothing.4 He told them, 'You also go and work in my vineyard, and I will pay you whatever is right.'5 So they went. "He went out again about noon and about three in the afternoon and did the same thing.6 About five in the afternoon he went out and found still others standing around. He asked them, 'Why have you been standing here all day long doing nothing?'7 "'Because no one has hired us,' they answered. "He said to them, 'You also go and work in my vineyard.' 8 "When evening came, the owner of the vineyard said to his foreman, 'Call the workers and pay them their wages, beginning with the last ones hired and going on to the first.' 9 "The workers who were hired about five in the afternoon came and each received a denarius. 10 So when those came who were hired first, they expected to receive more. But each one of them also received a denarius. 11 When they received it, they began to grumble against the landowner. 12 'These who were hired last worked only one hour,' they said, 'and you have made them equal to us who have borne the burden of the work and the heat of the day.' 13 "But he answered one of them, 'I

am not being unfair to you, friend. Didn't you agree to work for a denarius? 14 Take your pay and go. I want to give the one who was hired last the same as I gave you. 15 Don't I have the right to do what I want with my own money? Or are you envious because I am generous?'16 "So the last will be first, and the first will be last." **Matthew 20:1-16 (NIV2011)**

40 And if anyone wants to sue you and take your shirt, hand over your coat as well. 41 If anyone forces you to go one mile, go with them two miles. **Matthew 5:40-41 (NIV2011)**

1 "At that time Michael, the great prince who protects your people, will arise. There will be a time of distress such as has not happened from the beginning of nations until then. But at that time your people—everyone whose name is found written in the book—will be delivered. 2 Multitudes who sleep in the dust of the earth will awake: some to everlasting life, others to shame and everlasting contempt. **Daniel 12:1-2 (NIV2011)**

1 In the fifteenth year of the reign of Tiberius Caesar—when Pontius Pilate was governor of Judea, Herod tetrarch of Galilee, his brother Philip tetrarch of Iturea and Traconitis, and Lysanias tetrarch of Abilene—2 during the high-priesthood of Annas and Caiaphas, the word of God came to John son of Zechariah in the wilderness. 3 He went into all the country around the Jordan, preaching a baptism of repentance for the forgiveness of sins. **Luke 3:1-3 (NIV2011)**

25 During Solomon's lifetime Judah and Israel, from Dan to Beersheba, lived in safety, everyone under their own vine and under their own fig tree.**1 Kings 4:25 (NIV2011)**

34 Jesus spoke all these things to the crowd in parables; he did not say anything to them without using a parable. 35 So was fulfilled what was spoken through the prophet: "I will open my mouth in parables, I will utter things hidden since the creation of the world." **Matthew 13:34-35 (NIV2011)**

28 All the people in the synagogue were furious when they heard this. 29 They got up, drove him out of the town (Nazareth), and took him to the brow of the hill on which the town was built, in order to throw him off the cliff. 30 But he walked right through the crowd and went on his way. **Luke 4:28-30 (NIV2011)**

22 "His master replied, 'I will judge you by your own words, you wicked servant! You knew, did you, that I am a hard man, taking out what I did not put in, and reaping what I did not sow? 23 Why then didn't you put my money on deposit, so that when I came back, I could have collected it with interest?' **Luke 19:22-23 (NIV2011)**

Biblical Characters Who Are A Part Of Season 4 Episode 5

Pharisees & Sadducees

The Pharisees and Sadducees are actual groups of people in the bible who do conspire against Jesus and are recorded in Scriptures as having meetings to plot ways in which to trap meetings. The Scriptures do not record the events we see in this episode, and they are there to serve the author's literary purposes.

Sanhedrin

The Sanhedrin is an actual body of people recorded in the Scriptures, and it is the body that Jesus will eventually stand trial before being turned over to the Romans. The Scriptures do not record the events we see in this episode, and they are there to serve the author's literary purposes.

Joanna

Joanna is a woman in the Scriptures who supported Jesus and the disciples out of her own means. The Scriptures do not tell us exactly how she did it or how often, but she is presented as a woman of some financial means. The delivery of the box to the disciples is not recorded in Scripture and is there to serve the author's literary purposes.

The Disciples

The disciples are recorded in the Scriptures as having joined Jesus at the house of Lazarus, Mary, and Martha. The Scriptures do not record the event of the followers of Jesus being forced to go a second mile by the Romans, however Jesus did instruct them to do so in his teachings. The event is there to serve the author's literary purposes.

Lazarus, Martha, & Mary

Lazarus, Martha, & Mary who recorded in the Scriptures as hosting a meal for Jesus and his disciples. The episode accurately displays the roles of Mary and Martha during the meal as wells as Jesus' response to the women's behavior.

Mary

Jesus' mother Mary does appear several times with him in the gospels, but none of the role she plays in this episode with Jesus is found in the Scriptures. Their conversation is there to serve the author's literary purposes.

Judas

Judas is the keeper of the money bag for Jesus and the others as recorded in the Scriptures. The Scriptures do not record Judas going off to meet his former mentor and being influenced by him. The meeting is there to serve the author's literary purposes.

Jesus

Jesus does travel to Bethany to visit the home of Martha, Mary & Lazarus in the Scriptures. He does commend both Mary and Martha as the episode shows it. The Scriptures do not record a visit with his mother. It does not appear from the Scriptures that Jesus gave the parable of the workers in the home of Mary and Martha. Yet it can't be completely ruled out because it does appear Jesus was on his way to Jerusalem when it was spoken. The Scriptures do record Jesus' teachings on going the second mile, however there is nothing in Scripture that records Jesus and his disciples actually being forced to fulfill it by Roman soldiers. The Scriptures do not record the conversations between Judas and Jesus. This event is there to serve the author's literary purposes.

Bible Study Discussion Questions For Season 4 Episode 5

1. When was a time you went the extra mile for someone, and it really was not convenient for your to do so? How did you feel as you were doing it?

2. Have you ever had God send you a blessing out of nowhere to meet your financial need? What causes us to not trust that God will provide?

3. How do you think our wealth or our poverty may cause us to see a false gospel?

4. What do you think the followers of Jesus were most concerned about in the scene where the Romans forced them to carry their equipment for a mile?

5. Why do we have such a hard time with being humiliated by others? What do you think Jesus wants our response to be?

6. Do you tend to be more of a Mary or Martha in your walk with the Lord? Why do you think that is so?

7. Jesus was both truly God and truly human. What in this episode caused you to see his humanity in a way you had not seen before?

8. Do you think the members of the church ever behave like the members of the Sanhedrin? If so, how so?

9. If you had of been Jesus, would you have been tempted to heal Lazarus of his sickness when you saw him in pain at the party?

10. What's your understanding of Jesus's statement," the first shall be last, and the last shall be first?"

11. Why do you think Judas is having such a hard time with the way Jesus is going about building his kingdom?

12. Is there anything that causes you to question God's way of doing things?

13. What's the biggest mistake that you think Judas makes in this episode and why?

14. What was the point of having the story line of Mary being out in the woods picking berries?

15. Do you think Rabbi Joseph feels as though he has made the right choice to come to Jerusalem? Have you ever wanted to help in a situation, but didn't know what to do? How do you feel at that point?

6 RESOURCES FOR SEASON 4 EPISODE 6

Main Characters

Feast of Dedication—The Jewish Feast of Dedication, known as Hanukkah or Chanukah, commemorates the rededication of the Second Temple in Jerusalem during the second century BCE. This event followed the successful Maccabean Revolt against the Seleucid Empire, which sought to impose Hellenistic culture and religion on the Jewish people.

Big James—The disciple of Jesus who suffers a blow to his head.

Matthew & John—The disciples who exchange gifts related to their recordings of the gospels of Matthew and John.

Jesus—The Messiah and leader of the disciples who teaches the group and confronts the religious leaders with his claims.

Judas—The disciple of Jesus who is constantly seeking ways to increase the funding for the ministry of Jesus.

Matthew—The disciple who confronts Judas on the appearance of missing funds from the money bag.

Rabbi Joseph—The Pharisee on the Sanhedrin who wants to

protect Jesus.

Thomas—The disciple still in grief over his fiancée's death from months earlier. He is willing to speak up concerning the gravity of Jesus' decisions to go back to Jerusalem.

Peter—The disciple often trying to comfort Thomas.

Jairus—The synagogue administrator who is a follower of Jesus and sends a message to warn Jesus and the others of a plot to kill Jesus.

Zebedee—The father of James & John and deliverer of a message from Capernaum.

Summary of Season 4 Episode 6

The scene opens with a flashback. The followers of Jesus come rushing into a room. Big James has been injured with a blow to his head. All of them have been fleeing a dangerous situation and are soaking wet. As they lay Big James on the table to take care of his needs, Jesus finds a note at the end of the table with a message concerning Lazarus.

The scene then goes back to a period seven days prior to the opening of the episode. Jesus and his followers are celebrating the Feast of Dedication. Jesus is telling the story of the Maccabean Revolt, and the disciples are acting out the part as the story is being told. It begins with Alexander the Great and ends with the victory of the Maccabees. They are lighting the eight candles as the story is told for each of the days involved. They quote Scriptures together as part of the Feast of Dedication.

The disciples exchange gifts with each other. Matthew and John are both recording the events of Jesus's life. Matthew gives John parchment as a gift so that he can continue his writings on Jesus, and John gives Matthew a new stylus for him to continue his writings on the teachings and events of Jesus. Jesus and his followers sing songs together and quote Scripture together. As part of the festivities, John and Andrew have an arm-wrestling contest and to everyone's surprise, Andrew wins the battle. The scene closes with Mary and Tamar challenging each other.

Jesus makes the announcement that they will go to Jerusalem, and he will give a sermon on the final day of the Feast. A sense of gloom and doom falls over the group. When Jesus questions the mood, all begin to say that yes it will be a good thing to do except for Thomas. Thomas reminds them of the truth of the hostile reception they will probably receive.

The scene switches to James, Andrew, John & Matthew. They are thinking of a gift they could get for Thomas that could possibly lift his spirit. They agree to purchase him some sandals that were made for walking on long trips. Thomas currently has some expensive sandals that were made for standing, not walking. As they think about the amount of money left in the treasury bag to see if they can afford them, Matthew notices not all the coins are present in the bag.

Matthew goes to Judas to request funds for Thomas' gift. Judas balks at the idea of paying for new sandals for Thomas. He prefers Thomas sell the sandals he has and use the money to buy sandals made for walking. Matthew asks Judas where is the second money bag, and Judas insists there is no second bag. Matthew confronts Judas on the missing funds. Judas at first tries to blame it on extra expenses. Matthew does not buy it, and Judas becomes very defensive. Judas then explains that the work Jesus is doing is moving inefficiently and slowly. He is doing what he can to make sure they do not run out of funds before Jesus gets the chance to preach his message to the crowds. Matthew leaves the situation bewildered. He tells the others that they may have to barter to get money for the sandals. They jokingly ask if Judas was being stingy with the funds.

The scene switches to Rabbi Joseph. He is looking at scrolls and is writing a letter. His father comes in to see him. They have a great reconciling talk with each other with his father telling him how proud he is of his son. Rabbi Joseph confuses his father with Jesus' parable on prayer with the illustration of the snake and stone. He makes a strange request of his father when he says, "Don't give up on me Abba." He then says, "No matter how it goes in Sanhedrin, trust me that I love God, and I will always be faithful." His father assures him of his confidence in his son.

The scene switches to Thomas, Peter, James, John, and Andrew in the marketplace. Peter's job is to distract Thomas while the others go and search for the gift for Thomas. Peter uses the opportunity to try to get Thomas to open up about his feelings. Even though months have passed, Thomas is still in deep grief. The only time he doesn't feel bad is when he is involved in doing something important that takes his thoughts elsewhere. Peter tells him that it's not wrong to question, but it is wrong to not accept the answer. Thomas can't get pass why Jesus didn't do something to stop Rhema's death. Peter tried quoting the passage on God's thoughts and ways being different from ours, but Thomas finds little comfort in the verses.

Rabbi Joseph has sent a message to Jairus in Capernaum about the plot to kill Jesus. He wants Jairus to get the message to Jesus or his disciples to warn him not to go to Jerusalem. Jairus wonders who he can trust with the message.

The scene shifts to Jesus and the disciples quoting Scriptures together. Thomas does get the new gift of sandals that were made for walking. He's grateful for them. A lady gives Jesus a message that had been dropped off coming from Bethany on the other side of the Jordan. The disciples notice that Jesus is disturbed. Jesus lets them know that Lazarus is very sick. They are reassured when Jesus tells them that is a sickness that will not lead to death. Jesus leaves the room, and the disciples continue to have an uplifting time, singing the Song of Mariam. Jesus seems very troubled as he lay in bed.

The followers of Jesus are going through the grinding process of making flour. Judas comes to them with an idea of how they could make money faster. They could set up donation centers in each of the villages they go to, and people could make ongoing donations to the ministry. A person could be chosen to oversee the collections and bring the money to Jesus at a designated time. Then instead of spending time making flour, they could be out spreading the message of Jesus. The disciples question the practicality of his plan. Some feel as though there is a purpose in making the flour themselves by hand. There is a time and a season for everything, and now is a time for making flour.

Judas is discouraged by their lack of support for his idea. John attempts to talk to Judas about how our own ambitions can sometimes cloudy our understanding of the ministry of Jesus. What we think may be a plan to further the kingdom of God might actually be a cloak to move ahead with our own plans. Judas is not moved by his reasoning. He's certain his plan would be of benefit to Jesus. He's simply trying to be creative with the gifts given to him by God.

Judas attempts to tell Jesus about his plan. He tells Jesus that all he wants is to see his kingdom come and to remove any obstacles in the way. He even includes Jesus words to be as "gentle as doves, but also wise as serpents" as justification for his plan. Jesus asks has Joanna's donations run out. Judas responds they're close to running out, and that with the holidays, now would be a great time to set up donation points in various villages. Jesus lets Judas know that his vision for the world is bigger than anything Judas can dream. He also tells him to pay close attention to the sermon he will be preaching and the feelings inside of him as he hears the message. Jesus offers Judas no support for his collection plan.

Jairus calls in Zebedee, the father of James and John, in order for him to take the message himself to his sons. Jairus is afraid to trust anyone else with the message for fear it might get back to the Sanhedrin. Zebedee agrees to go and as a cover, he tells his wife that he is taking some of his oil to the temple for a possible contract. He has a letter of recommendation from Jairus to the officials in Jerusalem.

Jesus goes back to Jerusalem with his followers. Thomas looks bewildered over the decision. They cross the Jordan. Jesus heads to a group of sheep in a pen. He starts teaching on sheep recognizing the voice of the shepherd. He speaks on others coming before him who were thieves and robbers. Jesus sits on the steps to the temple to teach the disciples. Many people are simply walking past ignoring Jesus altogether. The Pharisees who are listening to his message become very agitated and challenge what he is saying. The disciples ask for an explanation of Jesus' teachings. Jesus' explanation infuriates the Pharisees even more.

Jesus emphasizes he is laying down his life and will take it up again. Judas gets very upset with the religious leaders over the insults they are hurling at Jesus. Judas is listening more to the religious leaders than he is to Jesus. Simon the Zealot encourages Judas to come back and ignore them. Jesus does not back down from the Pharisees but gets in their face with the claims he makes about himself and his Father. They threaten to stone Jesus, to which he questioned them as to which good work did they seek to stone Him. They claim it's not because of any good works, but because of his claims about his Father.

Once Jesus declares that he is in the Father and the Father is in him, the religious leaders begin picking up stones and throwing them at him and his followers. Big James is injured with a blow to the head. They run from the temple and out of Jerusalem to safety. They have to cross the Jordan without a boat so they all get soaking wet.

They bring John into the house and put him on the table. The episode is now at the point in the story as it was at the beginning of the episode. Jesus sees a note on the table. The note says that Lazarus is dead. The disciples are confused because Jesus had said the sickness would not end in death. When Jesus announces plans to go back to Bethany, they try to talk him out of it. Jesus tells them, he was glad that he was not there so that they will believe.

Zebedee arrives and wonders what has happened. Big James assures him that He is okay. Jesus disciples are confused over the state that Lazarus is actually in because Jesus talks of him being asleep and of him being dead. Jesus tells them to change clothes and prepare to leave in the morning. Thomas says they should go and die with him. When Zebedee is alone with James and John, he delivers the message on the plot to kill Jesus. He warns them that things are about to get a lot worse than the stoning attempt they recently experienced.

Scriptures Woven Into Season 4 Episode 6

1 Now a man named Lazarus was sick. He was from Bethany, the village of Mary and her sister Martha. 2 (This Mary, whose brother Lazarus now lay sick, was the same one who poured perfume on the Lord and wiped his feet with her hair.) 3 So the sisters sent word to Jesus, "Lord, the one you love is sick." **John 11:1-3 (NIV2011)**

16 "I am sending you out like sheep among wolves. Therefore be as shrewd as snakes and as innocent as doves. **Matthew 10:16 (NIV2011)**

4 When he heard this, Jesus said, "This sickness will not end in death. No, it is for God's glory so that God's Son may be glorified through it." 5 Now Jesus loved Martha and her sister and Lazarus. 6 So when he heard that Lazarus was sick, he stayed where he was two more days, 7 and then he said to his disciples, "Let us go back to Judea." 8 "But Rabbi," they said, "a short while ago the Jews there tried to stone you, and yet you are going back?" 9 Jesus answered, "Are there not twelve hours of daylight? Anyone who walks in the daytime will not stumble, for they see by this world's light. 10 It is when a person walks at night that they stumble, for they have no light." 11 After he had said this, he went on to tell them, "Our friend Lazarus has fallen asleep; but I am going there to wake him up." 12 His disciples replied, "Lord, if he sleeps, he will get better." 13 Jesus had been speaking of his death, but his disciples thought he meant natural sleep. 14 So then he told them plainly, "Lazarus is dead, 15 and for your sake I am glad I was not there, so that you may believe. But let us go to him." 16 Then Thomas (also known as Didymus) said to the rest of the disciples, "Let us also go, that we may die with him." **John 11:4-16 (NIV2011)**

1 There is a time for everything, and a season for every activity under the heavens: **Ecclesiastes 3:1 (NIV2011)**

1 "Very truly I tell you Pharisees, anyone who does not enter the sheep pen by the gate, but climbs in by some other way, is a thief and a robber. 2 The one who enters by the gate is the shepherd of the sheep. 3 The gatekeeper opens the gate for him, and the sheep listen to his voice. He calls his own sheep by name and leads them out. 4 When he has brought out all his own, he goes on ahead of them, and his sheep follow him because they know his voice. 5 But they will never follow a stranger; in fact, they will run away from him because they do not recognize a stranger's voice." 6 Jesus used this figure of speech, but the Pharisees did not understand what he was telling them. **John 10:1-6 (NIV2011)**

9 "So I say to you: Ask and it will be given to you; seek and you will find; knock and the door will be opened to you. 10 For everyone who asks receives; the one who seeks finds; and to the one who knocks, the door will be opened. 11 "Which of you fathers, if your son asks for a fish, will give him a snake instead? 12 Or if he asks for an egg, will give him a scorpion? 13 If you then, though you are evil, know how to give good gifts to your children, how much more will your Father in heaven give the Holy Spirit to those who ask him!" **Luke 11:9-13 (NIV2011)**

7 Therefore Jesus said again, "Very truly I tell you, I am the gate for the sheep. 8 All who have come before me are thieves and robbers, but the sheep have not listened to them. 9 I am the gate; whoever enters through me will be saved. They will come in and go out, and find pasture. 10 The thief comes only to steal and kill and destroy; I have come that they may have life, and have it to the

full. 11 "I am the good shepherd. The good shepherd lays down his life for the sheep. 12 The hired hand is not the shepherd and does not own the sheep. So when he sees the wolf coming, he abandons the sheep and runs away. Then the wolf attacks the flock and scatters it. 13 The man runs away because he is a hired hand and cares nothing for the sheep. 14 "I am the good shepherd; I know my sheep and my sheep know me— 15 just as the Father knows me and I know the Father—and I lay down my life for the sheep. 16 I have other sheep that are not of this sheep pen. I must bring them also. They too will listen to my voice, and there shall be one flock and one shepherd. 17 The reason my Father loves me is that I lay down my life—only to take it up again. 18 No one takes it from me, but I lay it down of my own accord. I have authority to lay it down and authority to take it up again. This command I received from my Father." 19 The Jews who heard these words were again divided. **John 10:7-19 (NIV2011)**

1 Praise the LORD. Praise the LORD, you his servants; praise the name of the LORD. 2 Let the name of the LORD be praised, both now and forevermore. 3 From the rising of the sun to the place where it sets, the name of the LORD is to be praised. 4 The LORD is exalted over all the nations, his glory above the heavens. 5 Who is like the LORD our God, the One who sits enthroned on high, 6 who stoops down to look on the heavens and the earth? **Psalm 113:1-6 (NIV2011)**

22 Then came the Festival of Dedication at Jerusalem. It was winter, 23 and Jesus was in the temple courts walking in Solomon's Colonnade. 24 The Jews who were there gathered around him, saying, "How long will you keep us in suspense? If you are the Messiah, tell us plainly." 25 Jesus answered, "I did tell you, but you do not believe. The works I do in my Father's name

testify about me, 26 but you do not believe because you are not my sheep. 27 My sheep listen to my voice; I know them, and they follow me. 28 I give them eternal life, and they shall never perish; no one will snatch them out of my hand. 29 My Father, who has given them to me, is greater than all; no one can snatch them out of my Father's hand. 30 I and the Father are one**." John 10:22-30 (NIV2011)**

8 It is better to take refuge in the LORD than to trust in humans. 9 It is better to take refuge in the LORD than to trust in princes. **Psalm 118:8-9 (NIV2011)**

31 Again his Jewish opponents picked up stones to stone him, 32 but Jesus said to them, "I have shown you many good works from the Father. For which of these do you stone me?" 33 "We are not stoning you for any good work," they replied, "but for blasphemy, because you, a mere man, claim to be God." **John 10:31-33 (NIV2011)**

15 Precious in the sight of the LORD is the death of his faithful servants. **Psalm 116:15 (NIV2011)**

27 He will confirm a covenant with many for one 'seven.' In the middle of the 'seven' he will put an end to sacrifice and offering. And at the temple he will set up an abomination that causes desolation, until the end that is decreed is poured out on him." **Daniel 9:27 (NIV2011)**

17 I will sacrifice a thank offering to you and call on the name of the LORD. **Psalm 116:17 (NIV2011)**

8 "For my thoughts are not your thoughts, neither are your ways my ways," declares the LORD. **Isaiah 55:8 (NIV2011)**

1Not to us, LORD, not to us but to your name be the glory, because of your love and faithfulness. 2 Why do the nations say, "Where is their God?" 3 Our God is in heaven; he does whatever pleases him. **Psalm 115:1-3 (NIV2011)**

Then sang Moses and the children of Israel this song unto the LORD, and spake, saying, I will sing unto the LORD, for he hath triumphed gloriously: the horse and his rider hath he thrown into the sea. **Exodus 15:1-2 (KJV)**

Biblical Characters Who Are A Part Of Season 4 Episode 6

The Disciples

The Disciples are recorded in the Scriptures as following Jesus into Jerusalem and the other side of the Jordan to hear his teachings Jesus does tell them that Lazarus is dead and that he was glad he was not there so that they could believe. The Scriptures do not record how the disciples of Jesus celebrated The Feast Of Dedication, do not record the disciples being struck as part of the stoning attempt against Jesus, do not record the exchanging of gifts among themselves, and do not record the making of the flour. The conversations with Judas by all of the disciples are also not a part of the Scriptures. All of these events are for the author's literary purposes.

Thomas

Thomas is an actual biblical character and the Scriptures do record him as saying let us go and die with him in reference to Jesus, but all of his actions centered around the loss of Rhema including his talks with Peter are not found in the Scriptures. They are in the episode for the author's literary purposes.

Judas

Judas is an actual biblical character, however none of his conversations and plans in this episode are found in the Scriptures. They are in the episode for the author's literary purposes.

Jairus

Jairus is an actual biblical character, however none of his conversations and actions in this episode are found in the Scriptures. They are in the episode for the author's literary purposes.

Zebedee

Zebedee is an actual biblical character and the father of James and John. All of the roles he plays in this episode are there for the author's literary purposes. None of them are recorded in the Scriptures.

Jesus

Jesus is an actual biblical character. The Scriptures do not record Jesus celebrating the Feast of Dedication with his disciples as displayed in the episode. The story leading up to the Feast of Dedication is true history. The Scriptures also do not record the conversations between Jesus and Judas. Almost all of the words in Jesus' sermon in Jerusalem can be found in the Scriptures. Jesus and the religious leaders did engage in debate over who Jesus truly is. The religious leaders did at one time pick up stones to stone Jesus, but the Scriptures do not record anyone actually being struck by the stones. Jesus does receive word about Lazarus being sick and his eventual death. The Scriptures do record Jesus' words to the disciples on going back to Bethany and that the sickness would not lead to death.

Bible Study Discussion Questions For Season 4
Episode 6

1. Have you ever had what you thought was a good plan, but you were not able to get anyone else to want to go along with it? How did you handle the rejection of it?

2. Would you have been eager to follow Jesus into Jerusalem after his warnings of the terrible things that would happen to him in Jerusalem? Why or why not?

3. Do you think Matthew should have told the others about his suspicions that some of the money was missing from the treasury? Why do you think he simply let the matter drop after his confrontation with Judas?

4. Why do you think Rabbi Joseph tells his father, "No matter what happens in the Sanhedrin don't give up on me. Trust me that I love God, and I will always be faithful."

5. What can cause us to be sincere in our desire to please God, and yet be outside of the will of God for our lives?

6. What were the different reactions of the people as Jesus sat on the temple steps teaching? How are they similar to what we find in the world today?

7. What claims of Jesus got him in the most trouble with the religious leaders?

8. Do you think there was anything sinful about the plan Judas had to increase the amount of money in the treasury? Why or why not?

9. What comfort do you find in Jesus' words that no one can snatch his followers out of his hands?

10. Why do you think Jesus just doesn't just reach out and heal Big James of his injury as he lies on the table?

11. Do you think it's easier to be a follower of Christ now than it would have been if you were right there among the disciples? Why or why not?

12. What do you think is at the heart of the words of Isaiah 55:8 "For my thoughts are not your thoughts, neither are your ways my ways," declares the LORD. Isaiah 55:8 (NIV2011)

13. Why do you think Jesus told the disciples that He was glad that He was not there when Lazarus died?

14. Why do you think the author included the scene of Jesus' followers making flour?

15. What do you think is Jesus emotional state at the end of this episode?

7 Resources For Season 4 Episode 7

Main Characters

Mary Magdelene—One of Jesus' followers who decides to write an account of what Jesus has done for her.

Matthew—One of Jesus' disciples who will eventually write the gospel of Matthew.

Lazarus—A friend of Jesus who has died, and he is the brother of Mary and Martha.

Little James—One of Jesus' disciples who walks with a limp and has increasing pain as he walks.

Thomas—One of Jesus' disciples whose fiancée was killed, and Jesus did nothing to stop her from dying.

Big James—One of Jesus' disciples who was struck in the head with a rock during the attempted stoning of Jesus.

Peter—One of Jesus' disciples who has begun to take a leadership role among the disciples.

Judas—One of Jesus' disciples who wants to see Jesus take a more active role in declaring himself the Messiah to the people.

Arnal—Lazarus' former business partner before he died.

Mary and Martha—Close friends of Jesus and the sisters of Lazarus who has died.

Jesus—The Son of God who raises Lazarus from the dead and warns of the dangers that are waiting for Him in Jerusalem.

Summary of Season 4 Episode 7

Episode 7 begins in a time period many years after the resurrection of Jesus Christ. The scene is a man riding on a carriage out in the wilderness. The man pays his fare to the cart owner and begins a journey up a steep hill to a cave. It turns out the man traveling is the disciple, Matthew. He has gone on a journey to bring Mary Magdalene some news good and bad. Although they are thrilled to see each other, he comes with mixed news.

The bad news is that Little James has been martyred in Egypt leaving behind his wife and daughters. The good news is that he has finished his gospel account and wants Mary to read over it first. Matthew discovers Mary has been doing some writings of her own. Her writings are for personal reasons to remind her of the darkness that Jesus brought her out. She's been having dreams of the darker times in her life.

The scene then shifts back to the present time of Episode 6 in which Jesus has told the disciples to prepare to go back to Bethany because Lazarus has died. Simon the Zealot is cutting branches from a tree to make walking canes for Big James and Little James, both of whom were injured in the stoning in the previous episode. Little James has been in considerable pain throughout his walk with Jesus, and the pain is growing much worse since the stoning incident. As the disciples all gather together, Jesus comes out and leads the group forward.

The next scene is of the followers of Jesus walking together in pairs along the road enroute to Bethany. Thomas and John are walking together. John is interested in knowing what Thomas meant when he said, "Let's go and die with him" after Jesus had mentioned going back to Bethany. The discussion gets heavy because Thomas actually wants to go and die because of the pain in him not only over the death of his fiancée Rhema, but also because Jesus did nothing to stop her death. John tries to comfort Thomas by mentioning the admonition to choose death over life from the book of Deuteronomy. But Thomas is not moved and insists that we are forced to accept that death is a part of life.

Peter and Big James are walking together, and Big James is recovering from the attempted stoning of Jesus. He had been struck in the head and wounded. Big James wants to bring up the topic of Jairus daughter being raised from the dead, but Peter does not want to discuss it. They debate what Jesus meant when he said that he would wake Lazarus up. Peter accuses Big James of trying to make things too simple, but James counters with "Pain has a way of flattening thigs out.

Judas and Nathaniel are walking together, and Judas inquires as to what things were like before he arrived. Nathaniel points out things were much quieter before they were famous or infamous depending on the perspective. Judas is confused that they seem to keep on losing in the struggle to make Jesus known to the world. He wants others to see Jesus' glory. Nathaniel reminds him that only Jesus knows what true glory looks like. Judas is convinced that were they are experiencing is certainly not what glory should look like.

Little James and Mary Magdalene are walking together. They discuss the issue of suffering as related to the psalm which asks the question, "How long, how long oh Lord have you forgotten me forever." Little James discusses the irony of Jesus giving him the power to heal others, while he himself is in constant pain that is getting even worse. They discuss, "If Jesus raises Lazarus from the dead, won't it raise bigger questions?" Little James asks Mary, "Is this what you expected." Mary shares the constant darkness she experienced before Jesus. She admitted that the darkness does return, but now it is the exception and not the rule in her life. She is grateful where God has brought her from. Her perspective on life has been gained by torment. They share memories of the first time they met and shared a meal together.

The scene switches to Lazarus' home. Mary, Jesus' mother, is holding Mary, Lazarus's sister in comfort. Martha is in grief crying. Lazarus' business partner, Arnal, from Jerusalem comes to comfort her. The family lawyer arrives to let them know that Lazarus had all his affairs in order and had left considerable wealth for them to be taken care of including the care of Jesus' mother. He gives them a key to a safe in the home where Lazarus had a considerable amount of money but that most of his money was in the banks. He also informs them that he was to give a message that "He" is coming"

Martha goes out to meet Jesus and shares her grief. She tells Jesus, if he had been there, her brother would not have died, and even now, whatever he asks from God, God will do. She asks for Jesus to either give them hope or relief. When Jesus tells her that her brother will rise again, she immediately assumes the general resurrection, but Jesus says that He is the resurrection and the life. The disciples are listening to Jesus talk to Martha, and Thomas is having a very difficult time accepting Jesus' words. Martha tells Jesus, even what I don't understand, I still believe. Jesus tells her to go and get her sister.

The disciples are not sure what Jesus meant by his words. Matthew and Peter approach Jesus asking if they were supposed to understand what his words meant. Jesus tells them, "not yet." Thomas is becoming increasingly upset.

Mary gets up to go to Jesus, and all the people in the house get up and follow here because they thing she is going outside to grieve more. Mary also tells Jesus that if he had been there her brother would not have died. She wants to know why Jesus did not come when they sent for him, and why did he wait. Jesus asks where have you laid him.

Jesus then looks at his mother, his disciples, and the people and begins to weep. He sobs uncontrollably as he falls down and his mother comes to hold him. The disciples, Mary and Martha are all confused. They never expected anything like this to come from Jesus. The disciples are wondering if Jesus is angry and upset with him. They start asking each other questions until Peter puts a stop to it.

In the next scene, the crowd is heading toward Lazarus tomb. They stop at the tomb. Jesus has to give the command three times before the disciples and Zebedee act to role the stone away. Martha reminds Jesus of the odor that will be present since he's been dead four days. When they roll away the stone, the odor does come out. Jesus prays to the Father, "Father, I thank you that you have heard me. I know that you always hear me. I am saying this on account of the people standing around, that they may believe that you sent me." The disciples talk amount themselves that they already believe in him, but Mary points out not all of them for the same things.

Jesus calls for Lazarus to come out. Lazarus comes out of the tomb. Some people scream upon seeing him, all are in shock and amazed. Jesus orders them to take off the burial clothes. Martha unbinds him. Mary hugs him and Jesus embraces him. Jesus tells Lazarus, "I'm sorry it had to be this way, but also not. There is a higher plan for it.

A Sadducee runs back to Jerusalem to report what Jesus did. There is also a spy of sorts he leaves the scene and rushes to tell someone. Big James wants to know why Jesus did this in front of everyone. Jesus lets him know it is because 'the time has come." Judas thinks the resurrection of Lazarus will unite the religious leaders behind Jesus and Jesus kingdom will be established. Thomas is angry and explodes on Jesus. Why do this for Lazarus, and not for Rhema or John the Baptist? Jesus tells him that God's plans for his kingdom can be crushing for others as well as for Jesus himself. The disciples attempt to comfort Thomas to no avail. Jesus knows his actions will get him into trouble with the Sadducees.

After everyone else leaves, Mary Magdalene remains at the empty tomb of Jesus. It is as though she has a premonition that she will be at another tomb, witnessing the same kind of action. She touches the stone that has been rolled away and looks at the burial clothes on the ground. She even looks inside the tomb.

The scene goes to Lazarus and his sister. It appears his resurrection body has some of the old pains in it as his body did before death. Jesus comes to see Lazarus. The scene shifts to Mary and Martha at a table. Mary stares at Martha as they are sitting. She cannot believe that Martha is sitting down at a table that needs to be cleaned and cleared. They also discuss what they could possibly give to Jesus to show their appreciation and thanks for what he has done.

The scene goes back to Jesus and Lazarus. Jesus lets his friend know that he is running out of time and that this would be his last public sign. He is honest with Lazarus about his future and the series of events that are being touched off by the religious leaders. Jesus has told the disciples three times what will happen in Jerusalem concerning him but they will not hear it. Lazarus has a difficult time hearing it himself. Jesus is frustrated with disciples, angry at the religious leaders for twisting his words, and dreading the cup of suffering that is awaiting him. He and Lazarus quote parts of Isaiah 53 together. Their discussion is interrupted by Thomas breaking things in another room.

The disciples have a discussion among themselves about what all of this means. They wonder why did Jesus not just speak a word from a distance. They wonder if this is the beginning of an army. They wonder if Thomas will stay the course. Judas sets off a firestorm when he says Thomas might not be among the true sheep. Little James has some severe pain come from within his body. Peter encourages them all to just go to bed and get some sleep.

The scene then switches back to the future in which the scene opened. As Mary reads from her writings about light verses darkness, several scenes from the present time pass by quickly such as Lazarus holding his burial clothes, Jesus being reported to members of the Sanhedrin, Mary getting money from a safe, Peter wrapping Big James' bandage, Little James writhing in pain, Thomas taking his wedding gift from Rhema out of a draw, Mary blowing out a candle, and Jesus picking up the broken pieces of the pottery that Thomas had smashed in anger. Mary ends her writing with metaphors of the bitter and the sweet they had experienced wishing there could have been another way.

Scriptures Woven Into Season 4 Episode 7

[1] After this, Jesus traveled about from one town and village to another, proclaiming the good news of the kingdom of God. The Twelve were with him, [2] and also some women who had been cured of evil spirits and diseases: Mary (called Magdalene) from whom seven demons had come out; [3] Joanna the wife of Chuza, the manager of Herod's household; Susanna; and many others. These women were helping to support them out of their own means. **Luke 8:1-3 (NIV2011)**

[9] When Jesus rose early on the first day of the week, he appeared first to Mary Magdalene, out of whom he had driven seven demons. **Mark 16:9 (NIV2011)**

[39] "Abraham is our father," they answered. "If you were Abraham's children," said Jesus, "then you would do what Abraham did. [40] As it is, you are looking for a way to kill me, a man who has told you the truth that I heard from God. Abraham did not do such things. [41] You are doing the works of your own father." "We are not illegitimate children," they protested. "The only Father we have is God himself." **John 8:39-41 (NIV2011)**

[54] Jesus replied, "If I glorify myself, my glory means nothing. My Father, whom you claim as your God, is the one who glorifies me. [55] Though you do not know him, I know him. If I said I did not, I would be a liar like you, but I do know him and obey his word. [56] Your father Abraham rejoiced at the thought of seeing my day; he saw it and was glad." [57] "You are not yet fifty years old," they said to him, "and you have seen Abraham!" [58] "Very truly I tell you," Jesus answered, "before Abraham was born, I am!" [59] At this, they picked up stones to stone him, but Jesus hid himself, slipping away from the temple grounds. **John 8:54-59 (NIV2011)**

[1] Now a man named Lazarus was sick. He was from Bethany, the village of Mary and her sister Martha. [2] (This Mary, whose brother Lazarus now lay sick, was the same one who poured perfume on

the Lord and wiped his feet with her hair.) ³ So the sisters sent word to Jesus, "Lord, the one you love is sick." ⁴ When he heard this, Jesus said, "This sickness will not end in death. No, it is for God's glory so that God's Son may be glorified through it." ⁵ Now Jesus loved Martha and her sister and Lazarus. ⁶ So when he heard that Lazarus was sick, he stayed where he was two more days, ⁷ and then he said to his disciples, "Let us go back to Judea." ⁸ "But Rabbi," they said, "a short while ago the Jews there tried to stone you, and yet you are going back?" **John 11:1-8 (NIV2011)**

¹¹ After he had said this, he went on to tell them, "Our friend Lazarus has fallen asleep; but I am going there to wake him up." ¹² His disciples replied, "Lord, if he sleeps, he will get better." ¹³ Jesus had been speaking of his death, but his disciples thought he meant natural sleep. ¹⁴ So then he told them plainly, "Lazarus is dead, **John 11:11-14 (NIV2011)**

¹⁶ Then Thomas (also known as Didymus) said to the rest of the disciples, "Let us also go, that we may die with him." **John 11:16 (NIV2011)**

¹⁷ On his arrival, Jesus found that Lazarus had already been in the tomb for four days. ¹⁸ Now Bethany was less than two miles from Jerusalem, ¹⁹ and many Jews had come to Martha and Mary to comfort them in the loss of their brother. ²⁰ When Martha heard that Jesus was coming, she went out to meet him, but Mary stayed at home. ²¹ "Lord," Martha said to Jesus, "if you had been here, my brother would not have died. ²² But I know that even now God will give you whatever you ask." ²³ Jesus said to her, "Your brother will rise again." ²⁴ Martha answered, "I know he will rise again in the resurrection at the last day." ²⁵ Jesus said to her, "I am the resurrection and the life. The one who believes in me will live, even though they die; **John 11:17-25 (NIV2011)**

²⁸ After she had said this, she went back and called her sister Mary aside. "The Teacher is here," she said, "and is asking for you." ²⁹ When Mary heard this, she got up quickly and went to him. ³⁰ Now

Jesus had not yet entered the village, but was still at the place where Martha had met him. [31] When the Jews who had been with Mary in the house, comforting her, noticed how quickly she got up and went out, they followed her, supposing she was going to the tomb to mourn there. [32] When Mary reached the place where Jesus was and saw him, she fell at his feet and said, "Lord, if you had been here, my brother would not have died." [33] When Jesus saw her weeping, and the Jews who had come along with her also weeping, he was deeply moved in spirit and troubled. [34] "Where have you laid him?" he asked. "Come and see, Lord," they replied. **John 11:28-34 (NIV2011)**

[35] Jesus wept. **John 11:35 (NIV2011)**

[36] Then the Jews said, "See how he loved him!" [37] But some of them said, "Could not he who opened the eyes of the blind man have kept this man from dying?" **John 11:36-37 (NIV2011)**

[38] Jesus, once more deeply moved, came to the tomb. It was a cave with a stone laid across the entrance. [39] "Take away the stone," he said. "But, Lord," said Martha, the sister of the dead man, "by this time there is a bad odor, for he has been there four days." [40] Then Jesus said, "Did I not tell you that if you believe, you will see the glory of God?" [41] So they took away the stone. Then Jesus looked up and said, "Father, I thank you that you have heard me. [42] I knew that you always hear me, but I said this for the benefit of the people standing here, that they may believe that you sent me." [43] When he had said this, Jesus called in a loud voice, "Lazarus, come out!" [44] The dead man came out, his hands and feet wrapped with strips of linen, and a cloth around his face. Jesus said to them, "Take off the grave clothes and let him go." **John 11:38-44 (NIV2011)**

[45] Therefore many of the Jews who had come to visit Mary, and had seen what Jesus did, believed in him. [46] But some of them went to the Pharisees and told them what Jesus had done. [47] Then the chief priests and the Pharisees called a meeting of the Sanhedrin.

"What are we accomplishing?" they asked. "Here is this man performing many signs. [48] If we let him go on like this, everyone will believe in him, and then the Romans will come and take away both our temple and our nation." **John 11:45-48 (NIV2011)**

Now when Jesus returned, a crowd welcomed him, for they were all expecting him. [41] Then a man named Jairus, a synagogue leader, came and fell at Jesus' feet, pleading with him to come to his house [42] because his only daughter, a girl of about twelve, was dying. As Jesus was on his way, the crowds almost crushed him. [43] And a woman was there who had been subject to bleeding for twelve years, but no one could heal her. **Luke 8:35-43 (NIV2011)**

[49] While Jesus was still speaking, someone came from the house of Jairus, the synagogue leader. "Your daughter is dead," he said. "Don't bother the teacher anymore." [50] Hearing this, Jesus said to Jairus, "Don't be afraid; just believe, and she will be healed." [51] When he arrived at the house of Jairus, he did not let anyone go in with him except Peter, John and James, and the child's father and mother. [52] Meanwhile, all the people were wailing and mourning for her. "Stop wailing," Jesus said. "She is not dead but asleep." [53] They laughed at him, knowing that she was dead. [54] But he took her by the hand and said, "My child, get up!" [55] Her spirit returned, and at once she stood up. Then Jesus told them to give her something to eat. [56] Her parents were astonished, but he ordered them not to tell anyone what had happened. **Luke 8:49-56 (NIV2011)**

How long, LORD? Will you forget me forever? How long will you hide your face from me? [2] How long must I wrestle with my thoughts and day after day have sorrow in my heart? How long will my enemy triumph over me? [3] Look on me and answer, LORD my God. Give light to my eyes, or I will sleep in death, [4] and my enemy will say, "I have overcome him," and my foes will rejoice when I fall. [5] But I trust in your unfailing love; my heart rejoices in your salvation. [6] I will sing the LORD's praise, for he has been good to me. **Psalm 13:1-6 (NIV2011)**

[1] When Jesus had called the Twelve together, he gave them power and authority to drive out all demons and to cure diseases, [2] and he sent them out to proclaim the kingdom of God and to heal the sick. [3] He told them: "Take nothing for the journey—no staff, no bag, no bread, no money, no extra shirt. [4] Whatever house you enter, stay there until you leave that town. [5] If people do not welcome you, leave their town and shake the dust off your feet as a testimony against them." [6] So they set out and went from village to village, proclaiming the good news and healing people everywhere. **Luke 9:1-6 (NIV2011)**

[54] Therefore Jesus no longer moved about publicly among the people of Judea. Instead he withdrew to a region near the wilderness, to a village called Ephraim, where he stayed with his disciples. [55] When it was almost time for the Jewish Passover, many went up from the country to Jerusalem for their ceremonial cleansing before the Passover. [56] They kept looking for Jesus, and as they stood in the temple courts they asked one another, "What do you think? Isn't he coming to the festival at all?" [57] But the chief priests and the Pharisees had given orders that anyone who found out where Jesus was should report it so that they might arrest him. **John 11:54-57 (NIV2011)**

[38] As Jesus and his disciples were on their way, he came to a village where a woman named Martha opened her home to him. [39] She had a sister called Mary, who sat at the Lord's feet listening to what he said. [40] But Martha was distracted by all the preparations that had to be made. She came to him and asked, "Lord, don't you care that my sister has left me to do the work by myself? Tell her to help me!" [41] "Martha, Martha," the Lord answered, "you are worried and upset about many things, [42] but few things are needed—or indeed only one. Mary has chosen what is better, and it will not be taken away from her." **Luke 10:38-42 (NIV2011)**

[1] Who has believed our message and to whom has the arm of the LORD been revealed? [2] He grew up before him like a tender shoot,

and like a root out of dry ground. He had no beauty or majesty to attract us to him, nothing in his appearance that we should desire him. [3] He was despised and rejected by mankind, a man of suffering, and familiar with pain. Like one from whom people hide their faces he was despised, and we held him in low esteem. [4] Surely, he took up our pain and bore our suffering, yet we considered him punished by God, stricken by him, and afflicted. [5] But he was pierced for our transgressions, he was crushed for our iniquities; the punishment that brought us peace was on him, and by his wounds we are healed. [6] We all, like sheep, have gone astray, each of us has turned to our own way; and the LORD has laid on him the iniquity of us all. [7] He was oppressed and afflicted, yet he did not open his mouth; he was led like a lamb to the slaughter, and as a sheep before its shearers is silent, so he did not open his mouth. [8] By oppression and judgment he was taken away. Yet who of his generation protested? For he was cut off from the land of the living; for the transgression of my people, he was punished. [9] He was assigned a grave with the wicked, and with the rich in his death, though he had done no violence, nor was any deceit in his mouth. [10] Yet it was the LORD's will to crush him and cause him to suffer, and though the LORD makes his life an offering for sin, he will see his offspring and prolong his days, and the will of the LORD will prosper in his hand. [11] After he has suffered, he will see the light of life and be satisfied; by his knowledge my righteous servant will justify many, and he will bear their iniquities. [12] Therefore I will give him a portion among the great, and he will divide the spoils with the strong, because he poured out his life unto death, and was numbered with the transgressors. For he bore the sin of many, and made intercession for the transgressors. **Isaiah 53:1-12 (NIV2011)**

[25] Jesus answered, "I did tell you, but you do not believe. The works I do in my Father's name testify about me, [26] but you do not believe because you are not my sheep. [27] My sheep listen to my voice; I know them, and they follow me. [28] I give them eternal life, and they shall never perish; no one will snatch them out of my hand. [29] My Father, who has given them to me, is greater than all; no one can snatch them out of my Father's hand. [30] I and the Father

are   one."
John 10:25-30 (NIV2011)

Biblical Characters Who Are A Part Of Season 4
Episode 7

The Disciples

The Disciples are recorded in Scripture as accompanying Jesus to Bethany and being present at the raising of Lazarus from the dead. However, the conversations around Thomas and his grief are not a part of the Scriptures and neither are the disciples' conversations on the possible resurrection of Lazarus from the dead. These conversations are for the author's literary purpose.

Matthew and Mary

Matthew and Mary are recorded in the Scriptures. Matthew is historically believed to be the author of the gospel of Matthew. There are no historical records indicating that Mary wrote about her experiences. These events are for the author's literary purpose.

Mary and Martha

Mary and Martha are recorded in the Scriptures as being sisters and the brother of Lazarus. The words that Mary and Martha speak to Jesus when he arrives at the funeral are recorded in the Scriptures as well as Martha's words at the tomb. The other conversations they have are part of the author's literary purpose.

Judas

Judas is recorded in Scripture as being the treasurer for the disciples. None of the conversations involving Judas are found in the Scriptures. They are part of the author's literary purpose.

Lazarus

Lazarus is recorded in the Scripture as being raised from the dead by Jesus almost exactly as depicted in the episode. None of the conversations involving Lazarus are found in the Scriptures. They are part of the author's literary purpose.

Thomas

Thomas is recorded in the Scriptures as saying to the other disciples, "Let go die with him." None of the other conversations are recorded nor is there a mention of his fiancée dying. They are part of the author's literary purpose.

Mary (The Mother Of Jesus)

Mary is recorded in the Scriptures as the mother of Jesus. None of the conversations of Mary with anyone in the episode is included in the Scriptures. There also is not any indication that Mary lived with Martha, Mary, and Lazarus. The events are part of the author's literary purpose.

Little James

Little James is one of the disciples recorded in the Scriptures, but the Scriptures do not indicate that he walked with a limp or was in constant pain. These events are part of the author's literary purpose.

Jesus

Jesus is recorded in the Scripture as going to Bethany to raise Lazarus from the dead. The episode portrays the resurrection exactly as Scripture indicates. Jesus' words to Mary and Martha upon his arrival are almost verbatim Scripture. Jesus does indeed weep. Jesus is aware that the religious leaders are plotting against him. The Scriptures do not record Jesus' conversation with

Thomas, Lazarus, his mother, Matthew or Peter in this episode. Those conversations are for the author's literary purposes.

Bible Study Discussion Questions For Season 4 Episode 7

1. Has there ever been a time in your life in which you were somewhat nervous that if God did not answer a particular person's prayers, that person might leave the faith?

2. The episode opens with mention of Little James having been killed in Egypt for his faith. How would you feel if somebody very close to you was martyred for their faith?

3. Mary and Martha both say to Jesus, "If you had been here, my brother would not have died." Is this a statement of faith, blame, or anger? Why do you think so?

4. Little James is confused that Jesus has given him the power to heal everyone except for himself. God used Paul to do many miracles including healings. Trophimus was one of his closest traveling companions and coworkers in the

Lord. Yet we find this verse, "Erastus stayed in Corinth, and I left Trophimus sick in Miletus." 2 Timothy 4:20. How do you think Paul felt leaving his close friend sick? How do you think Trophimus felt?

5. Thomas wants to die over the loss of Rhema. When is it proper for a Christian to genuinely long to die?

6. Little James asked Mary about following Jesus, "Is this what you expected?" In what way has following Jesus been different from what you expected?

7. What does it mean to you to know that Jesus is the resurrection and the life?

8. What was your initial reaction to seeing Jesus breaking down and crying? Is this what you had imagined before when you read the verse "Jesus wept."

9. Jesus tells his disciples, "I am glad for your sake that I was not there, so that you may believe." Why would Jesus make this statement to a group of people who already believe in Him?

10. What do you think your reaction would have been to Lazarus coming out of the tomb?

11. How would you answer Thomas' question, "why did you do this for Lazarus, but not for Rhema or for John your own cousin?" When was a time you felt like Thomas?

12. Jesus makes the statement that God's plans can be crushing for others as well as for Jesus Himself. What do you think Jesus is trying to convey with these words?

13. Jesus is very frustrated with the disciples over their refusal to accept what he says will happen in Jerusalem. Why do you think it is so difficult for them to receive this message from him?

14. Why does the raising of Lazarus from the dead present a problem for the disciples? How does it show God can't be kept in a neat little box?

15. What do you think is the reason for the author showing Mary Magdalene alone at the tomb?

8 RESOURCES FOR SEASON 4 EPISODE 8

Main Characters

King David & Abigail—They are characters from the Old Testament. David & Abigail are married, and they celebrate a victory over the Ammonites.

Jesse—The brother of Simon the Zealot and is the man Jesus healed who had been lame at the pool of Bethesda.

Veronica—The woman Jesus had healed when she touched the hem of his garment.

Pontius Pilate—The governor Ceasar had appointed over Judea.

Atticus—Roman military figure who seeks to protect Rome's interests at all cost and is often seeing spying on Jesus and the disciples.

Caiaphas—The Jewish high priest and the leader of the Sanhedrin.

Mary—The sister of Martha and Lazarus who anoints Jesus with some very expensive ointment.

Rabbi Joseph—A member of the Sanhedrin who believes in Jesus and wants to protect him.

Rabbi Shmuel—A member of the Sanhedrin who wants to make sure that Jesus gets a fair hearing at the Sanhedrin.

Arnal—Lazarus' business partner who brings the two rabbis to see Jesus.

Judas—The disciple who is removing money from the treasury and complains of Mary wasting money on Jesus.

King Herod—The king of the Jews in Judea. He is the tool Caiaphas hopes to use to get rid of Jesus.

Lazarus—The person Jesus raised from the dead.

Joanna—A follower of Jesus who helps support the ministry financially. Her husband Chuza is a member of Herod's court.

Simon The Zealot (Z) And Matthew—The two disciples Jesus sends into the city to get a donkey for Jesus to ride upon into Jerusalem.

The Disciples—The followers of Jesus who continue to accompany him on his journey toward Jesus.

Jesus—The Son of God who teaches on the kingdom of God and takes out a harness that has passed on from his father who received it from his father to generations back to King David.

Summary of Season 4 Episode 8

The episode opens with a scene from the Old Testament. King David is marching triumphantly on his horse into the city of Jerusalem. The people are waving palms and shouting "Hosanna to the King." David arrives into the city victorious over the Ammonites. He goes in to see his wife Abigail and their son Daniel. David and Abigail explain the feast of the Passover to their son. David takes his son out and chooses the perfect lamb that is to be sacrificed. David points out to his son to makes sure to anoint the feet of the sacrificial lamb. They tell the story of how the Israelites had to leave in haste out of Egypt. David gives his son the bridle from the horse that he rode upon as he entered Jerusalem victoriously. That bridle would be passed down from son to son through the generations.

The scene switches to Jerusalem. Jesse, the lame man who was healed at the pool of Bethesda and is also the brother of Simon the Zealot, and Veronica, the woman who had been healed from twelve years of suffering from a blood flow, are preaching telling others about Jesus. A member of the Sadducees is challenging them by casting doubt on everything they claim about Jesus. They are aware of the religious leaders attempt to stone Jesus earlier and calls them out on it.

The next scene involved Pontius Pilate and Atticus talking to each other. The discussion involves the large number of Jews coming to Passover this year because of Jesus. Pilate is concerned Tiberius Caesar did not send in more troops. Atticus informs him it might be a test of a Pilate's leadership. Pilate brings up the issue of Lazarus thinking it may be nothing more than Jewish imagination. Atticus is not sure what to think of it, because of the many things he has observed Jesus doing. Pilate is beginning to get nervous. Both men agree that Caiaphas the high priest is already spooked by the people and their beliefs about Jesus.

The scene goes to Mary, the sister of Lazarus. She enters the shop to purchase a perfume ointment for the greatest of kings. The shop owner keeps trying to sell her the cheaper perfumes until Mary starts pulling out bags of money. She pays a year's wages for the entire bottle of the most expensive perfume for the one she believes to be the most important king the world has ever known. The shop owner is dumbfounded by Mary's actions.

The scene goes to a raging debate in the Sanhedrin over the resurrection of Lazarus. Some want Jesus removed immediately. Rabbi Joseph calls for an inquiry to see if Jesus had really been raised from the dead because if so, Jesus might be Elijah. Rabbi Shmuel asks for permission to go and talk with Jesus to study if he might be Elijah. The Sanhedrin is afraid of losing power if all the people continue to believe in Him. Caiaphas, the high priest, speaks of a prophecy he has received of one many dying for the people so that the nation will survive. He says perhaps Jesus is the man. But his death has to be done in a very public way and only the Romans could make that happen. Caiaphas has a plan to use King Herod to get Jesus in trouble with Rome. He is going to send a letter to King Herod who was on his way to Jerusalem for the Feast.

Rabbi Shmuel and Rabbi Joseph express their disappointment with the motives and actions of members of the Sanhedrin. Rabbi Shmuel wants to talk with Jesus to discover what his motives are so that he can help Jesus. Rabbi Joseph is already a believer in Jesus and wants to protect Jesus from the Sanhedrin. He thinks the Sanhedrin is beyond being rational about Jesus. Rabbi Joseph's father is Arnal, who is Lazarus' business partner. They use this connection to try to find Jesus for a face-to-face interview.

The scene shifts to the city of Capernaum. The people are preparing to leave the city to make the journey to Jerusalem to celebrate the Passover. Jairus is taking along passengers for the trip which include Salome, James' and John's mother, along with Eden, Peter's wife. Gaius, the Roman Praetor whose son Jesus healed, asks them to give greetings to Peter, Jesus, and Matthew. The message to Peter is Shalom, Shalom. The message to Jesus is one of gratitude and love from him and his full family. The message to Matthew is to take care of Himself. Eden invites Gaius to join them on the trip. He declines the offer for several reasons. Shula and Barnabus arrive just before Jarius takes off. They were friends of Jesus who had been healed by Jesus early in his ministry.

The next scene involves Judas rising up early and taking some of the money from the general purse to his own little bag and entering a ledger to hide his theft. He sees Thomas leaving and going somewhere with a shovel. He decides to secretly follow Thomas. Thomas goes to spot on the hill and digs a hole to bury the time clock that he was going to give to Rhema as part of her gift for the wedding day. The clock meant a lot to him because of his final personal time with Rhema before she was killed. Judas looks at what Thomas is doing, but stays hidden in the background.

The scene switches to the arrival of King Herod and Herodias into the city of Jerusalem. Joanna, Chuza and another woman is present. Herod receives the letter from Caiaphas the high priest. Herod is hoping for the chance to get to meet Jesus. He's heard about the miracles that Jesus has done.

The next scene is at the house of Lazarus. A big dinner has been planned in Lazarus' home and Jesus and the disciples are all present. There is a knock at the door and in come Arnal with Rabbi Shmuel and Rabbi Joseph. Arnal is very relieved at interrupting them once Jesus welcomes the rabbis and already knows them both. Jesus congratulates them on their appointment to seats on the Sanhedrin.

They try to tell Jesus that he is in danger from the highest levels of government and this is a matter of life and death. Rabbi Joseph, states that Lazarus's resurrection has caused things to escalate. Rabbi Shmuel wants to know what Jesus' plans are and whether or not he has an army of some sort. Jesus asks Rabbi Shmuel what he hopes for in the Messiah. Shmuel's hope is that the Messiah will usher in a new Davidic Kingdom, drive out the oppressors, restore justice and glory for Israel, and bring prosperity for all in a new golden age in which Israel will be a light to the world revealing God to all people. Shmuel is confused when Jesus asks him what his role will be in that new kingdom.

Jesus then contrasts that view with what it will be like when the Son of man comes in his glory with his angels with him. Jesus then tells the parable of the sheep and goats and the separation Jesus makes at the judgment. Jesus speaks of the hungry, the naked, the prisoners, the homeless and the thirsty as being the ones he identified with, and whatever was done for them, the least of these, was done for him. Rabbi Shmuel is confused that the Son of Man is identified with the lowest of all people. He thinks Jesus is minimizing the Torah requirements, the traditions, the sacrifices, and the feasts which are all so important to him. Jesus tries to tell him about Micah's words in his prophecy, "He has told you oh man what is good. And what does the Lord require of you but to do justice and to love kindness and to walk humbly before you God."

Rabbi Shmuel thinks Jesus is not observant enough of the traditions. Their discussion is interrupted by Mary entering the room with tears in her eyes bringing the very expensive bottle of perfume. She goes over and pours it on Jesus, feet and begin wiping his feet with her hair.

The fragrance fills the room. Judas is the first to recognize the financial value of the perfume and he goes berserk over the amount of money that has been wasted. The money could have been given to the poor or used for a host of other things. Rabbi Shmuel goes berserk over the act itself and the contradiction it is to what Jesus just said about helping the poor, in addition to the number of ritual rules the act itself broke concerning feet touching, head covering, and the titles Mary gave to Jesus. Jesus responded by saying the poor you will have with you always and you can always do good for them anytime you like, but you will not always have me. She has anointed my body for burial, and what she has done will be told in memory of her all over the world, wherever the gospel is preached.

Rabbi Shmuel is very disappointed with Jesus and recognizes there is nothing else he can do to help Jesus. Jesus realizes there is little else he can do to help Rabbi Shmuel. Shmuel leaves the house in anger. Judas tries to tell Jesus that he can't afford to alienate members of the Sanhedrin if they are to unite the people. Judas leaves the house and runs into Rabbi Shmuel who is still outside waiting for his companions. He and Judas have an exchange of words. Rabbi Shmuel wants to contact Judas in the future if possible. Rabbi Joseph leaves the house and tells Lazarus that he does not share Rabbi Shmuel's indignation.

The scene switches to Pilate's palace with Pilate, his wife, Herod, Herodias, Chuza, Cassandra, and Joanna. As a believer, Joanna listens very closely to all that is being said. Pilate teases Herod by saying the Jews have been saying this Jesus might be the new king. Herod fights back by informing him that he had received a letter from Caiaphas indicating Jesus might be organizing a rebellion on the level of the Maccabean uprising if it is shown he raised Lazarus from the dead. Pilate suggests that Lazarus be put to death to stop things from reaching an uprising of any kind.

The scene goes to Joanna and Pilate's wife having a discussion about faith, marriage, and paying a price for what you believe. Both of them feel that something big is about to happen.

The scene goes to James and John who are about to enjoy Martha's cinnamon cakes. They feel it is a slight betrayal of their mother to eat anyone else's cinnamon cakes. They are caught by surprise when Nathaniel arrives with their mother and Eden. They try to quickly get rid of the cakes.

Jesus sends Simon the Zealot and Matthew on a mission in a village to bring back a donkey that has never been ridden before. They are to tell the owner, "The Lord has need of it, and the person will release the donkey. They are sent on their way with Matthew having a ton of what ifs, but Simon the Zealot has faith in Jesus' word. Atticus, the Roman cohort, is spying on Jesus, and he follows the two disciples into the village.

Jesus' mother brings him a bag with a box inside of it. It's something he had received from Joseph. Jesus feels this is a way for the three of them to be together in this moment. He warns his mother, he can no longer shield her from the pain of his mission and maybe she should stay with Lazarus.

Simon and Matthew do find the colt Jesus requested and used Jesus' words. The person in charge gives him the donkey. Simon shares how the donkey will be used based on the prophecy in Zechariah indicating your Kings come to you riding on a donkey. As they leave with the donkey, the person giving them the donkey heads for Jerusalem with the news the king will be riding into the city and entering the eastern gate. Atticus follows him on another horse to see where he is headed.

The donkey is brought to Jesus. Jerusalem is filled with expectation. People start gathering palms. Joanna and Chuza are stuck in traffic with all the people getting involved with the palms. Joanna decides to leave Chuza forever and go to join the crowd to welcome in Jesus. She purchases palms to pass them out. Different people are seen looking at the excitement of the crowd including,

Pilate and his wife, Rabbi Joseph, Rabbi Shmuel, and Caiaphas.

Jesus takes a harness from the bag that was given to him by his father Joseph, who had received it from generations before of father passing it to sone. They prepare the donkey for Jesus. Jesus asks them to journey into Jerusalem with him because his time had come to do the will of his Father in heaven. Peter replies, Lord where else will we go. You alone have the words to eternal life. Jesus tells his followers, no matter what happens this week, no that I loved you as my own and I will love you to the end. Jesus starts to ride toward Jerusalem. They follow him, with all of their faces looking sad and downcast.

Scriptures Woven Into Season 4 Episode 8

[40] His servants went to Carmel and said to Abigail, "David has sent us to you to take you to become his wife." [41] She bowed down with her face to the ground and said, "I am your servant and am ready to serve you and wash the feet of my lord's servants." [42] Abigail quickly got on a donkey and, attended by her five female servants, went with David's messengers and became his wife. **1 Samuel 25:40-42 (NIV2011)**

[1] These were the sons of David born to him in Hebron: The firstborn was Amnon the son of Ahinoam of Jezreel; the second, Daniel the son of Abigail of Carmel; **1 Chronicles 3:1 (NIV2011)**

[1] The LORD said to Moses and Aaron in Egypt, [2] "This month is to be for you the first month, the first month of your year. [3] Tell the whole community of Israel that on the tenth day of this month each man is to take a lamb for his family, one for each household. [4] If any household is too small for a whole lamb, they must share one with their nearest neighbor, having taken into account the number of people there are. You are to determine the amount of lamb needed in accordance with what each person will eat. [5] The animals you choose must be year-old males without defect, and you may take them from the sheep or the goats. [6] Take care of them until the fourteenth day of the month, when all the members of the community of Israel must slaughter them at twilight. [7] Then they are to take some of the blood and put it on the sides and tops of the doorframes of the houses where they eat the lambs. [8] That same night they are to eat the meat roasted over the fire, along with bitter herbs, and bread made without yeast. [9] Do not eat the meat raw or boiled in water, but roast it over a fire—with the head, legs and internal organs. [10] Do not leave any of it till morning; if some is left till morning, you must burn it. [11] This is how you are to eat it: with your cloak tucked into your belt, your sandals on your feet and your staff in your hand. Eat it in haste; it is the LORD's Passover. [12] "On that same night I will pass through Egypt and strike down

every firstborn of both people and animals, and I will bring judgment on all the gods of Egypt. I am the LORD. **Exodus 12:1-12 (NIV2011)**

[26] And when your children ask you, 'What does this ceremony mean to you?' [27] then tell them, 'It is the Passover sacrifice to the LORD, who passed over the houses of the Israelites in Egypt and spared our homes when he struck down the Egyptians.' " Then the people bowed down and worshiped. [28] The Israelites did just what the LORD commanded Moses and Aaron. [29] At midnight the LORD struck down all the firstborn in Egypt, from the firstborn of Pharaoh, who sat on the throne, to the firstborn of the prisoner, who was in the dungeon, and the firstborn of all the livestock as well. [30] Pharaoh and all his officials and all the Egyptians got up during the night, and there was loud wailing in Egypt, for there was not a house without someone dead. [31] During the night Pharaoh summoned Moses and Aaron and said, "Up! Leave my people, you and the Israelites! Go, worship the LORD as you have requested. [32] Take your flocks and herds, as you have said, and go. And also bless me." [33] The Egyptians urged the people to hurry and leave the country. "For otherwise," they said, "we will all die!" [34] So the people took their dough before the yeast was added, and carried it on their shoulders in kneading troughs wrapped in clothing. [35] The Israelites did as Moses instructed and asked the Egyptians for articles of silver and gold and for clothing. [36] The LORD had made the Egyptians favorably disposed toward the people, and they gave them what they asked for; so they plundered the Egyptians. [37] The Israelites journeyed from Rameses to Sukkoth. There were about six hundred thousand men on foot, besides women and children. [38] Many other people went up with them, and also large droves of livestock, both flocks and herds. [39] With the dough the Israelites had brought from Egypt, they baked loaves of unleavened bread. The dough was without yeast because they had been driven out of Egypt and did not have time to prepare food for themselves. **Exodus 12:26-39 (NIV2011)**

[25] then kings who sit on David's throne will come through the gates of this city with their officials. They and their officials will come

riding in chariots and on horses, accompanied by the men of Judah and those living in Jerusalem, and this city will be inhabited forever. **Jeremiah 17:25 (NIV2011)**

[1] Six days before the Passover, Jesus came to Bethany, where Lazarus lived, whom Jesus had raised from the dead. [2] Here a dinner was given in Jesus' honor. Martha served, while Lazarus was among those reclining at the table with him. [3] Then Mary took about a pint of pure nard, an expensive perfume; she poured it on Jesus' feet and wiped his feet with her hair. And the house was filled with the fragrance of the perfume. [4] But one of his disciples, Judas Iscariot, who was later to betray him, objected, [5] "Why wasn't this perfume sold and the money given to the poor? It was worth a year's wages." [6] He did not say this because he cared about the poor but because he was a thief; as keeper of the money bag, he used to help himself to what was put into it. [7] "Leave her alone," Jesus replied. "It was intended that she should save this perfume for the day of my burial. [8] You will always have the poor among you, but you will not always have me." **John 12:1-8 (NIV2011)**

[9] Meanwhile a large crowd of Jews found out that Jesus was there and came, not only because of him but also to see Lazarus, whom he had raised from the dead. [10] So the chief priests made plans to kill Lazarus as well, [11] for on account of him many of the Jews were going over to Jesus and believing in him. **John 12:9-11 (NIV2011)**

[45] Therefore many of the Jews who had come to visit Mary, and had seen what Jesus did, believed in him. [46] But some of them went to the Pharisees and told them what Jesus had done. [47] Then the chief priests and the Pharisees called a meeting of the Sanhedrin. "What are we accomplishing?" they asked. "Here is this man performing many signs. [48] If we let him go on like this, everyone will believe in him, and then the Romans will come and take away both our temple and our nation." **John 11:45-48 (NIV2011)**

[49] Then one of them, named Caiaphas, who was high priest that

year, spoke up, "You know nothing at all! [50] You do not realize that it is better for you that one man die for the people than that the whole nation perish." [51] He did not say this on his own, but as high priest that year he prophesied that Jesus would die for the Jewish nation, [52] and not only for that nation but also for the scattered children of God, to bring them together and make them one. [53] So from that day on they plotted to take his life. **John 11:49-53 (NIV2011)**

[55] When it was almost time for the Jewish Passover, many went up from the country to Jerusalem for their ceremonial cleansing before the Passover. [56] They kept looking for Jesus, and as they stood in the temple courts they asked one another, "What do you think? Isn't he coming to the festival at all?" [57] But the chief priests and the Pharisees had given orders that anyone who found out where Jesus was should report it so that they might arrest him. **John 11:55-57 (NIV2011)**

[18] She said to Elijah, "What do you have against me, man of God? Did you come to remind me of my sin and kill my son?" [19] "Give me your son," Elijah replied. He took him from her arms, carried him to the upper room where he was staying, and laid him on his bed. [20] Then he cried out to the LORD, "LORD my God, have you brought tragedy even on this widow I am staying with, by causing her son to die?" [21] Then he stretched himself out on the boy three times and cried out to the LORD, "LORD my God, let this boy's life return to him!" [22] The LORD heard Elijah's cry, and the boy's life returned to him, and he lived. [23] Elijah picked up the child and carried him down from the room into the house. He gave him to his mother and said, "Look, your son is alive!" [24] Then the woman said to Elijah, "Now I know that you are a man of God and that the word of the LORD from your mouth is the truth." **1 Kings 17:18-24 (NIV2011)**

[22] Then came the Festival of Dedication at Jerusalem. It was winter, [23] and Jesus was in the temple courts walking in Solomon's Colonnade. [24] The Jews who were there gathered around him,

saying, "How long will you keep us in suspense? If you are the Messiah, tell us plainly." ²⁵ Jesus answered, "I did tell you, but you do not believe. The works I do in my Father's name testify about me, ²⁶ but you do not believe because you are not my sheep. ²⁷ My sheep listen to my voice; I know them, and they follow me. ²⁸ I give them eternal life, and they shall never perish; no one will snatch them out of my hand. ²⁹ My Father, who has given them to me, is greater than all; no one can snatch them out of my Father's hand. ³⁰ I and the Father are one." ³¹ Again his Jewish opponents picked up stones to stone him, ³² but Jesus said to them, "I have shown you many good works from the Father. For which of these do you stone me?" ³³ "We are not stoning you for any good work," they replied, "but for blasphemy, because you, a mere man, claim to be God." **John 10:22-33 (NIV2011)**

¹ Observe the month of Aviv and celebrate the Passover of the LORD your God, because in the month of Aviv he brought you out of Egypt by night. ² Sacrifice as the Passover to the LORD your God an animal from your flock or herd at the place the LORD will choose as a dwelling for his Name. ³ Do not eat it with bread made with yeast, but for seven days eat unleavened bread, the bread of affliction, because you left Egypt in haste—so that all the days of your life you may remember the time of your departure from Egypt. ⁴ Let no yeast be found in your possession in all your land for seven days. Do not let any of the meat you sacrifice on the evening of the first day remain until morning. ⁵ You must not sacrifice the Passover in any town the LORD your God gives you ⁶ except in the place he will choose as a dwelling for his Name. There you must sacrifice the Passover in the evening, when the sun goes down, on the anniversary of your departure from Egypt. **Deuteronomy 16:1-6 (NIV2011)**

³¹ "When the Son of Man comes in his glory, and all the angels with him, he will sit on his glorious throne. ³² All the nations will be gathered before him, and he will separate the people one from another as a shepherd separates the sheep from the goats. ³³ He will

put the sheep on his right and the goats on his left. [34] "Then the King will say to those on his right, 'Come, you who are blessed by my Father; take your inheritance, the kingdom prepared for you since the creation of the world. [35] For I was hungry and you gave me something to eat, I was thirsty and you gave me something to drink, I was a stranger and you invited me in, [36] I needed clothes and you clothed me, I was sick and you looked after me, I was in prison and you came to visit me.' [37] "Then the righteous will answer him, 'Lord, when did we see you hungry and feed you, or thirsty and give you something to drink? [38] When did we see you a stranger and invite you in, or needing clothes and clothe you? [39] When did we see you sick or in prison and go to visit you?' [40] "The King will reply, 'Truly I tell you, whatever you did for one of the least of these brothers and sisters of mine, you did for me.' [41] "Then he will say to those on his left, 'Depart from me, you who are cursed, into the eternal fire prepared for the devil and his angels. [42] For I was hungry and you gave me nothing to eat, I was thirsty and you gave me nothing to drink, [43] I was a stranger and you did not invite me in, I needed clothes and you did not clothe me, I was sick and in prison and you did not look after me.' [44] "They also will answer, 'Lord, when did we see you hungry or thirsty or a stranger or needing clothes or sick or in prison, and did not help you?' [45] "He will reply, 'Truly I tell you, whatever you did not do for one of the least of these, you did not do for me.' [46] "Then they will go away to eternal punishment, but the righteous to eternal life." **Matthew 25:31-46 (NIV2011)**

[6] With what shall I come before the LORD and bow down before the exalted God? Shall I come before him with burnt offerings, with calves a year old? [7] Will the LORD be pleased with thousands of rams, with ten thousand rivers of olive oil? Shall I offer my firstborn for my transgression, the fruit of my body for the sin of my soul? [8] He has shown you, O mortal, what is good. And what does the LORD require of you? To act justly and to love mercy and to walk humbly with your God. **Micah 6:6-8 (NIV2011)**

[44] Philip, like Andrew and Peter, was from the town of Bethsaida. [45] Philip found Nathanael and told him, "We have found the one

Moses wrote about in the Law, and about whom the prophets also wrote—Jesus of Nazareth, the son of Joseph." [46] "Nazareth! Can anything good come from there?" Nathanael asked. "Come and see," said Philip. **John 1:44-46 (NIV2011)**

[1] Now there were some present at that time who told Jesus about the Galileans whose blood Pilate had mixed with their sacrifices. [2] Jesus answered, "Do you think that these Galileans were worse sinners than all the other Galileans because they suffered this way? [3] I tell you, no! But unless you repent, you too will all perish. **Luke 13:1-3 (NIV2011)**

[28] After Jesus had said this, he went on ahead, going up to Jerusalem. [29] As he approached Bethphage and Bethany at the hill called the Mount of Olives, he sent two of his disciples, saying to them, [30] "Go to the village ahead of you, and as you enter it, you will find a colt tied there, which no one has ever ridden. Untie it and bring it here. [31] If anyone asks you, 'Why are you untying it?' say, 'The Lord needs it.' " [32] Those who were sent ahead went and found it just as he had told them. [33] As they were untying the colt, its owners asked them, "Why are you untying the colt?" [34] They replied, "The Lord needs it." [35] They brought it to Jesus, threw their cloaks on the colt and put Jesus on it. **Luke 19:28-35 (NIV2011)**

[68] Simon Peter answered him, "Lord, to whom shall we go? You have the words of eternal life. [69] We have come to believe and to know that you are the Holy One of God." **John 6:68-69 (NIV2011)**

[1] It was just before the Passover Festival. Jesus knew that the hour had come for him to leave this world and go to the Father. Having loved his own who were in the world, he loved them to the end. **John 13:1 (NIV2011)**

[9] Rejoice greatly, Daughter Zion! Shout, Daughter Jerusalem! See, your king comes to you, righteous and victorious, lowly and riding

on a donkey, on a colt, the foal of a donkey. **Zechariah 9:9 (NIV2011)**

Biblical Characters Who Are A Part Of Season 4 Episode 8

David, Abigail & Daniel

The Scriptures do record David and Abigail as being married, and they do have a son named Daniel. Although it is most likely that David celebrated the Passover and taught his son about it, The Scriptures do not give us an account of the events, nor does it give an account of David marching into the city with palms after defeating the Ammonites. The events in the episode are for the author's literary purposes.

Jesse (man healed at Bethesda) and Veronica (woman healed after touching the hem of Jesus' garment)

Neither Jesse or Veronica is named in the Scriptures, and the Scriptures do not record them teaming up and preaching to others about Jesus. Their roles in this episode are for the author's literary purposes.

Pontius Pilate & Herod

The Scriptures do record Pontius Pilate having a meeting with Herod, but it was after Jesus was arrested. The Scriptures do record Pontius and Herod not really liking each other as seen in the episode. The Scriptures do record that Herod was hoping for a chance to see Jesus. The Scriptures do not record the conversation that takes place between the men in this episode, and they do not record Herod receiving a letter from Caiaphas. The conversations and letter are for the author's literary purposes.

Mary, Martha & Lazarus

The Scriptures do record them as siblings, and that Lazarus was indeed raised from the dead. The Scriptures do record Mary anointing Jesus' feet with some very expensive perfume, but they do not provide any details on the actual purchase at the store. Mary was harshly rebuked for the use of the perfume by Judas and then commended by Jesus. Martha was serving at a dinner given in honor of Jesus, and Lazarus was present. The Scriptures do not record the presence of rabbis interrupting the dinner to question Jesus. All of the conversations regarding the unexpected guests are not found in the Scriptures as well as the conversations between the three siblings, but are there for the author's literary purposes.

Caiaphas

Caiaphas is recorded in the Scriptures as being the high priest, and the Scriptures do indicate that he prophesied that Jesus would die for the nation. The Scriptures do not record the other conversations of Caiaphas in this episode, and they are there for the author's literary purposes.

Jairus, Salome, and Eden (Peter's wife)

The Scriptures records each of these, but the Scriptures do not record them going to Jerusalem for the Passover nor do they record the conversations they have in Capernaum. These events are for the author's literary purposes.

The Disciples

The Scripture do record the presence of the disciples with Jesus when he was anointed by Mary. Jesus does send two of his disciples into a village to obtain a donkey for him to ride upon in Jerusalem. The two disciples are not named in the Scriptures but they are told to say, "The Lord needs it." Peter does make the declaration that there was nowhere to go because Jesus had the words to eternal life, however those words were spoken much earlier in Jesus' ministry after the feeding of the 5,000 in John's gospel. The disciples do prepare to march into Jerusalem with Jesus. The Scriptures do not record Salome coming to visit her sons James and John. The events are portrayed as they are for the author's literary purposes

Thomas

The Scriptures do record Thomas being present in Bethany, but they do not record any of the events related to his grief over Rhema. They are there for the author's literary purposes.

Judas

The Scriptures do record Judas stealing from the money belonging to the group. Judas does have an outburst over Mary using the perfume to anoint Jesus, and the event is recorded in Scripture as portrayed in the episode with a rebuke coming from Jesus. The Scriptures do not record Judas leaving the party early or of him engaging a member of the Sanhedrin after the meal. These events are there for the author's literary purposes.

Joanna & Pilate's wife

Both of these women are recorded in the Scriptures, but the Scriptures do not record any of the events portrayed by them in this episode. These events are for the author's literary purposes.

Jesus

The Scriptures do record that a banquet was hold in his honor and that he was anointed by Mary with some expensive perform. His words to those who rebuked Mary are identical to what's found in Scripture. The Scriptures do not record Jesus having members of the Sanhedrin as guests at the banquet with whom he discussed his teachings. The Scriptures do record Jesus speaking the parable of the Least Of These, but they are not specific as to when and where

Jesus spoke the parable. Jesus does warn his disciples of the difficult times awaiting him in Jerusalem. Jesus does send two of his disciples ahead of the group to locate and bring back a donkey based on the words, "The Lord has need of it." The Scriptures do record the people getting ready to receive Jesus with palm branches. The Scriptures do not record Mary, his mother, bringing him the gift of the bridle to be placed on the donkey nor of her presence outside of Jerusalem. There is nothing in Scripture about a bridle being passed down from King David to Jesus. This legend is for the author's literary purposes.

Bible Study Discussion Questions For Season 4
Episode 8

1. When in your life was there something you knew you had to do, but you dreaded it all the way to the end?

2. What do you think was the significance of King David pointing out to his son to anoint the feet of the sacrificial lamb?

3. With all that Atticus has seen Jesus do, why do you think he refuses to become a follower of Jesus? Why do some people refuse to believe.

4. What motivates Mary to purchase the perfume that she buys? Have you ever been motivated to do something similar?

5. Looking at the Sanhedrin, what happens when we gain to much power over others?

6. What change do you notice in Gaius? What change has someone noticed in you since you came to Christ?

7. What do you think Thomas is really doing in burying the time clock? Can you think of something in your own life you needed to bury before walking closer to the Lord?

8. Jesus challenged Rabbi Joseph on his expectations of the arrival of the Messiah. What are you really hoping for and expecting when Jesus returns?

9. What kind of help was Rabbi Joseph trying to provide to Jesus? Why didn't Jesus need his help?

10. Have you ever tried to help Jesus, only to discover Jesus is far bigger than you are?

11. Jesus says, "the poor you will have with you always." Is that a reason for us to put off doing something for the poor or an opportunity to do something now? How do you know when you have done enough for the poor?

12. What risk does Joanna take in her decision to go all out in following Jesus by jumping out of the carriage?

13. If Jesus sent you out to pick up a car at a car lot with the words, "If someone asks you why you're taking the car, tell them the Lord has need of it," how confident would you be in picking up the car?

14. Why do you think the author includes the scene with Jesus and his mother concerning the gift in the box even though it's not found in Scripture?

15. What was the mood of the disciples in the episode as Jesus prepared to ride toward Jerusalem? Is this how you imagined the ride would be launched on Palm Sunday before seeing the episode?

9 ABOUT THE AUTHOR

Rick Gillespie-Mobley came to know the Lord at age 17 in 1973. He has been a committed evangelical pastor since 1983 and retired at the end or 2021. He currently is a part of A Covenant Order Of Evangelical Presbyterians (ECO). He is a gifted communicator and uses stories and humor in his messages in a way that engages his audiences. He has an extensive Christian background in several Christian denominations that include charismatics, Methodists, Church of God In Christ, Full Gospel, United Church Of Christ, Assemblies of God, and Presbyterians.

Rick has a true love for the Scriptures as being the word of God and the authoritative interpretation for how we should live our lives today.

His background as a lawyer has given him a unique way of analyzing the text in addition to the way he learned at seminary. He has put together this guide to help people to find the richness in the Chosen Series. If one is not aware of the Scriptures, some of the things in the series will just zip past you. Rick has gathered the Scriptures referred to in each episode along with a summary of each episode to assist people in watching the series. The group discussion questions are designed to allow for almost anyone to lead a discussion on the series.

Rick was married on August 30, 1980 to his bride Toby. They served together as co-pastors for nearly 38 years. In addition to their adult children Marjoe (Rebecca), Samantha, Anita (Milan), Keon (Ashley), and Sharon, they have served as foster parents for 20 years. Rick is a graduate of Hornell Senior High School in Hornell, NY, Hamilton College B.A. in Clinton, NY, Gordon Conwel Theological Seminary M. Div. in S. Hamilton, MA, Trinity Bible College & Seminary D. Min in Newburgh, IN and Boston University School of Law J.D in Boston, MA.

Rick has served with his wife Toby as co-pastors of Roxbury Presbyterian Church (6 years) in Boston, Ma, and Glenville New Life Community Church (24 years).

They also served as pastors in Cleveland, Oh at New Life Fellowship (4 Years) in Cleveland, OH, Calvary Presbyterian Church (2 years), and New Life At Calvary (8 years). Toby was honorably retired in 2020 and Rick was honorably retired in 2021. Rick and Toby were both ordained in the Presbyterian Church of the United States Of America, but transferred their membership to A Covenant Order of Evangelical Presbyterian (ECO). Rick was admitted to practice law in both Massachusetts and Ohio.

10 OTHER BOOKS BY THE AUTHOR

Other books by Rick Gillespie-Mobley Include The Following:

20 Small Group Bible Studies

Easter Comes Alive

Why Can't A Woman Preach, Teach, Pastor Or Be An Apostle

Christmas: What Child Is This (Drama)

Five Mother's Day or Women's Day Sermons

Rich Black History Sermons: Africans In The Bible

The Play: Easter Comes Alive With The Resurrection

The Eye Of The Pastor: 11 Stories You Should Have Been Told Before You Started Ministry

Five Sermons For Father's Day Of Men's Day

Is God In The Crisis: From Triage To Transformation

Helpful Guide To Understanding "The Chosen" Season 1

Helpful Guide To Understanding "The Chosen" Season 2

Helpful Guide To Understanding "The Chosen" Season 3

Helpful Guide To Understanding "The Chosen" Season 4

The Practice Of The Presence Of God For Today's Youth. Brother Lawrence Speaks Today.

Growing In Christ Through The Book Of James: 12 Bible Studies

The Art Of Becoming Ushers and Greeters

The Art Of Writing A Eulogy

All of these books are available on Amazon.com, and a portion of each sell goes to Compassion International to help provide for the needs of children around the world and to ministry in Liberia.

Rick has an extensive collection of nearly 700 sermons located at sermoncentral.com which are free and readily available for use. Some are available in Spanish. Simply type his name in the Sermon Central search bar for the free resources. His sermons have been viewed over six million times.

Made in the USA
Las Vegas, NV
24 October 2024

10388231R00095